Table of Contents

Digital SAT®
5-Hour Quick Prep

by Ron Woldoff, MBA

with Jane Burstein

Digital SAT® 5-Hour Quick Prep For Dummies®

Published by: **John Wiley & Sons, Inc.,** 111 River Street, Hoboken, NJ 07030-5774, www.wiley.com

Copyright © 2024 by John Wiley & Sons, Inc., Hoboken, New Jersey

Published simultaneously in Canada

For general information on our other products and services, please contact our Customer Care Department within the U.S. at 877-762-2974, outside the U.S. at 317-572-3993, or fax 317-572-4002. For technical support, please visit https://hub.wiley.com/community/support/dummies.

Wiley publishes in a variety of print and electronic formats and by print-on-demand. Some material included with standard print versions of this book may not be included in e-books or in print-on-demand. If this book refers to media such as a CD or DVD that is not included in the version you purchased, you may download this material at http://booksupport.wiley.com. For more information about Wiley products, visit www.wiley.com.

Library of Congress Control Number: 2023949195

ISBN 978-1-394-23210-9 (pbk); ISBN 978-1-394-23211-6 (ebk); ISBN 978-1-394-23213-0 (ebk)

SKY10063511_122823

Start Here

The SAT challenges your ability to recall everything you studied in high school, some of which you probably haven't touched in years. Really all you need is a refresher, some strategies, and practice. *Digital SAT 5-Hour Test Prep For Dummies* has all that and more. It goes beyond rehashing what you've learned (and forgotten) by providing exam-specific strategies and tips for answering questions quickly and getting through the exam. It provides examples, practice questions, and an abridged practice exam to hone your test-taking skills, identify areas you need to work on, and build your confidence for taking the SAT. And it makes the process of preparing for the SAT as quick and painless as possible.

Succeeding on the SAT is like conquering any challenge: If you know what to do, and you practice, you'll be fine. I get you started with some review and guidance. The rest is up to you.

About This Book

Digital SAT 5-Hour Quick Prep For Dummies takes you on a whirlwind tour of the SAT. This book leads you through each section of the exam, explaining what the test-makers are looking for and how you can deliver it. It starts with a simple overview of how to sign up for the test and what the test covers; takes a deeper dive into the reading, writing, and math sections of the test, along with sample questions; and then challenges you with a shortened practice test. In the process, you discover how to approach the questions, avoid common mistakes, and master the intuitive tricks that help you knock it out of the park.

The book delivers all this in five study blocks equivalent to five hours of study. Depending on how much you know about each subject and how fast a test-taker you are, each block may take a little more or a little less time than promised, but the time promise gives you a general idea of how much time to allocate for each study block, so you can pace yourself appropriately.

Some study blocks are short, and others are long, depending on what you're trying to accomplish. Here's a rundown of what you'll find in each block and about how much time it's likely to take you to complete each one:

>> **Block 1 (20 minutes):** Find out what you need to know about registering for the SAT, exam rules and tips, the topics covered, and SAT scoring.

>> **Block 2 (1 hour):** Get up to speed on the reading and writing sections of the test, practice answering sentence-completion and critical-thinking questions, and pick up some test-taking strategies that can improve your score.

>> **Block 3 (2 hours):** Refresh your memory and build your math skills in topic areas including numbers and operations, algebra, geometry, trigonometry, statistics, and probability. Answer sample math questions and develop techniques for answering them faster and improving your chances when you have to guess.

>> **Block 4 (1 hour, 30 minutes):** This block contains an abridged practice test. By taking this practice test, you'll understand how to pace yourself and what content you need to review as you build confidence for taking the real SAT.

>> **Block 5 (10 minutes):** The shortest block in the book offers quick tips on what you can do the night before to improve your score on test day.

As you read through this book, you'll notice that some words have a style all their own. Each SAT vocabulary word in this text appears in *this font*, followed directly by its definition. Learning what words mean in context is one of the best ways to build vocabulary and is a great way to develop your ability to guess the meanings of unfamiliar words when you encounter them on the test.

Foolish Assumptions

I'm betting you picked up this book because you *have to* take the SAT as part of your college application process, but that's not the only foolish assumption I'm making about you. Here are the others:

>> You're committed to scoring high on the SAT and willing to invest the time and effort to achieve that goal.

>> You're busy and you don't want to waste your time with a bunch of fluff that isn't on the test.

>> You didn't goof off the entire time you were in high school, so you're familiar with secondary education curriculum as it relates to reading, writing, and arithmetic, but you may benefit from a little refresher in certain areas.

Icons Used in This Book

Icons are those cute little pictures that appear in the margins of this book. They indicate why you should pay special attention to the accompanying text. Here's how to decode them:

This icon points out helpful hints about strategy — what all-star test-takers know, and rookies need to learn.

This icon identifies the sand traps that the SAT writers are hoping you'll fall into as you take the test. Take note of these warnings so you know what to do (and what not to do) as you move from question to question on the real SAT.

When you see this icon, be sure to file away the information that accompanies it. The material will come in handy as you prepare for (and take) the SAT.

This icon indicates an example practice question within the regular chapter text.

Where to Go from Here

Get started! You have exactly what you need right here in your hands, so breathe deep and turn the page. You got this!

Block **1**

SAT Overview in 20 Minutes

The best and easiest way to reduce your anxiety and own the SAT is to become familiar with it. Knowing what to expect means you can plan for it, so nothing on exam day is a surprise.

This block covers SAT basics, including what's on the test; how it's structured; and when, where, and how often you should take it. You also find out how to prepare for the exam and how to interpret your score.

Signing Up for the SAT

The SAT is given at multiple times at select high schools and testing centers throughout the United States and in English-speaking schools in many other countries. This section explains how and when to register for an exam and the acceptable methods of payment.

Choosing when to take and retake the test

The SAT is typically offered seven times a year, and you can take it as often as you like. Ideally, you take it two or three times, but the door is open if you want another chance. Most high schoolers follow this pattern.

>> **Start in the fall of your sophomore year:** Take the PSAT/NMSQT, which stands for Preliminary SAT/National Merit Scholarship Qualifying Test, and is sort of a junior SAT. For you as a 10th grader, this exam doesn't count for much other than a practice run and eye-opener of the series of exams to come.

>> **Continue in the fall of your junior year:** Take the PSAT/NMSQT again, only this time it counts. If you do well, it opens the door to many scholarship opportunities and special programs.

>> **In the spring of your junior year:** Take the SAT as a practice test, though you can send in your scores if you're pleased with them. Note that you can also take an unscored practice exam, but this experience isn't quite the same as the real thing. Some juniors take the SAT twice during the spring.

>> **In the fall of your senior year:** Take the SAT again for real. This time you're ready, and you should do well enough to use these scores for your application. If you're an early decision candidate, take the test in October or November.

>> **In the winter of your senior year:** You have one more chance to get it right, or if you did get it right, you have one more chance to get that scholarship. By now you're a pro, so success is just one last test away.

REMEMBER

The SAT is typically given on a Saturday, but exceptions are made for those who can't test on Saturday for religious reasons. If you fall into that category, your SAT may be on a Sunday or a Wednesday following a Saturday SAT day. Get a letter from your religious leader on letterhead and mail it in with your registration form.

TIP

Register early to select a test site. When you register, you may request a test site, but if it's filled, you get an alternate. So don't delay — send in the form or register online as soon as you know when and where you want to take the exam. You'll probably want to test at your own high school, if possible, where the campus setting is familiar to you.

Requesting accommodations

Like many products and services, the SAT stresses fairness and equal access for all students, including those with special needs. Even if you think you don't belong in this category, skim this section. You may discover an option that will help you gain a test-taking advantage.

Learning disabilities

If you have a learning disability, you may be allowed to take the SAT under special conditions. The first step is to get an Eligibility Form from your school counselor. (Homeschoolers, call a local high school.) You may also want to ask your college counseling or guidance office for a copy of the *College Board Services for Students with Disabilities* brochure. If your school doesn't have one, contact the College Board directly or check the testing agency's website (`https://accommodations.collegeboard.org`).

TIP

Once you're certified for accommodations on any College Board test (an AP, an SAT Subject Test, or the PSAT/NMSQT), you're certified for all College Board tests, unless your need for accommodation arises from something temporary.

File the form well in advance of when you expect to take the test. If the College Board grants you the accommodation, you'll be eligible for extra time on the SAT, which could mean an extra 50 percent of time for each test. So, if a regular test-taker has 32 minutes per verbal module, for example, an extended-timer gets 48 minutes.

Physical issues

At no additional charge, the SAT also provides wheelchair accessibility, large-print tests, and other accommodations for students who need them. Be sure to submit your Eligibility Form early so that the College Board can request documentation and prepare your accommodations. You can send paper documentation or file an Eligibility Form online. Check out `https://accommodations.collegeboard.org` for details.

If a physical issue (say, a broken arm) occurs shortly before your scheduled SAT and you can't easily take the exam later, call College Board Customer Service, explain the situation, and have your physician fill out the forms requesting whatever accommodation you need.

TIP

Questions about special needs? Your high school's counselor or principal can help, or you can check the preceding link or email the College Board (ssd@info.collegeboard.org).

Getting financial help to cover fees

If you need financial help, you can apply for a fee waiver, available to low-income high school juniors and seniors who live in the United States, Puerto Rico, and other American territories. (United States citizens living in other countries may also be eligible for fee waivers.) The College Board also gives you four extra score reports for free, along with four request forms for college application fee waivers. The College Board does what it can.

You can also check with your school counselor for fee-waiver applications. (As with everything SAT, if you're a homeschooler, call a local high school for a form.) And be careful to avoid additional fees when you can. You run into extra charges for late or changed registration and for some extras — super-speedy scores, an analysis of your performance, and the like.

Registering for the test

You can register for the SAT online, by mail, or, if you've taken the SAT before, by phone.

Online registration is simple: Go to www.sat.collegeboard.org/register to create an account, sign up, and choose a test center and date. You need to have a credit card or PayPal account and a digital photo of yourself ready to upload. Be sure the photo meets the College Board's standards: a headshot where your whole face is visible and you're the only one in the photo. Head coverings are okay if they're religious in nature.

You can also register by mail. At the time of this writing, you must register by mail if you're younger than 13 or older than 21 or if you need to take the exam on a Sunday for religious reasons.

You can also ask your school guidance counselor for a registration form. If you're homeschooled, call the nearest public or private high school, or call the College Board Customer Service Center for help. If you register by mail, you'll have to attach a photo and enclose registration payment (credit card number, a check from a United States bank, or a bank draft).

The College Board Customer Service line within the U.S. is 866-756-7346 and outside the U.S. is 212-713-7789. Hearing-impaired test-takers can call the TTY Customer Service number, which within the U.S. is 888-857-2477 and outside the U.S. is 609-882-4118. You can also contact the College Board by mail at this address: College Board SSD Program, P.O. Box 8060, Mount Vernon, IL 62864-0060.

TIP

However you register, you'll be asked whether you want to sign up for the Student Search Service. Answer yes and fill out the questionnaire. Colleges, universities, and some scholarship-granting organizations receive information about you from this service. Expect lots of emails and letters — a little annoying, perhaps, but it's good to know that the schools are interested in you. You may also discover a school or scholarship that you weren't aware of but that meets your needs perfectly.

WARNING

Scammers are interested in you, too. Don't send personal or financial information to any organization unless you know it's legitimate. You know this, of course, but exam registration and college application is a new game. Not sure something is legit? Call the College Board Customer Service line to check.

Knowing What to Expect on the SAT

What are you getting into here? Well, it's nothing you can't handle, but knowing what's on the test and the knowledge and skills required to score well will help you to prepare more effectively and feel less anxious on test day. In this section, I explain what the test covers and how it's structured, point out a key difference between the paper and computer versions of the exam, and provide insight into the knowledge and abilities you will and will not be tested on.

What's on the SAT

Here is the digital SAT testing experience, in this order:

>> **Reading and Writing section:** Two 32-minute modules consisting of 27 questions each, totaling 64 minutes for 54 questions.

>> **10-minute break.**

>> **Math section:** Two 35-minute modules consisting of 22 questions each, totaling 70 minutes for 44 questions. You're provided with an on-screen calculator for both modules.

Within each module, each question counts the same toward your score: The more questions you get right, the higher your score for that module. An easy question is worth the same as a hard question. Because you can move back and forth within each section, one strategy is to skip around and answer all the easy questions first and then go back and work the hard questions. If you like this idea, *try it out on a practice test* before exam day.

Table 1-1 provides a quick overview of what's on the exam.

TABLE 1-1 ## Digital SAT Breakdown by Section

Section	Number of Questions	Time Allotted
Reading and Writing Module 1	27 questions	32 minutes
Reading and Writing Module 2	27 questions	32 minutes
Break	—	10 minutes
Math Module 1	22 questions	35 minutes
Math Module 2	22 questions	35 minutes

Each section mixes in a few unscored "trial" questions, which are impossible to discern from the actual, scored questions. This is good — it means you don't get an extra, unscored "trial" module.

Taking the adaptive (computer) test

On the computer version of the exam, the *second* Reading and Writing or Math module becomes easier or harder based on your performance on the *first* one. For example, if you do exceptionally well on the first Math module, the SAT thinks you're good at math, so it makes the second Math module harder. Even if you don't get as many right answers in the second Math module, your score will be higher than that of someone who bombs the first section and performs better in the second section.

Note that the paper-based practice SATs from CollegeBoard.org have more questions in each section (33 questions per Reading and Writing module; 27 questions per Math module), but no stated time limit. These practice SATs are excellent for preparing, but they don't reflect the actual testing experience.

Knowing what the SAT really looks for

The SAT attempts to measure the skills you need to succeed in school and in the workplace. It's not a measure of how smart you are, nor is it a measure of how well you do in school. It measures how adaptable you are, and especially how well you prepare for a major exam.

The SAT doesn't test facts you studied in school. You don't need to know when Columbus sailed the Atlantic or how to calculate the molecular weight of an atom. Instead, the SAT takes aim at your ability to follow a logical sequence to comprehend what you've read and to write grammatically well in Standard English. The math portion checks on the math skills you have picked up during your years in high school. The point is that the SAT isn't a giant final exam or a review of high school. It's a test of your *skills*, *not* your knowledge.

Use this to your advantage. The skills for the Reading and Writing section, covered in Block 2, are easy to learn and just take practice to master. The skills for the Math section are also of a limited scope and are captured in Block 3 of this book. In other words, pretty much everything you need to know for the SAT fits into a smallish book. There may be an occasional "oddball" question as the SAT steps outside its defined scope of topics, but these questions are very few and very far between.

Preparing to Take the SAT

As soon as you sign up for an SAT, the clock starts ticking. You have only so much time to study and practice, and suddenly the exam is tomorrow morning. The good news: I've led many students down this road, with great results, and here I've *curated* (collected) the best success strategies. Note that these strategies are *in addition* to studying with this book:

>> **Sign up for challenging courses in school.** Skip the courses that require papers short enough to tweet and just enough math to figure out how many minutes remain before your next vacation. Go for subjects that stretch your mind. Specifically, stick it out with math at least through Algebra II. If high school is in your rearview mirror, check out extension or enrichment adult-ed courses. Colleges will appreciate this initiative along with your SAT scores.

>> **Get into the habit of reading.** Instagram, TikTok, and YouTube don't do the trick. Instead, take on academic journals, established news sources, and any publication aimed toward an adult or college-level audience. The more you read challenging material, the more you build your ability to comprehend it. This will help you in so many ways in life, but on the SAT, it helps you understand vocabulary, analyze reasoning, and deconstruct evidence. Take note of unfamiliar words and check the words online. Also notice how an author makes a point — through description, citing experts, word choice, and so forth. This helps you understand the passages and writing methods of the Reading and Writing section.

>> **Develop a critical eye.** Read the school or local paper, websites, or any publication, and look for reasoning techniques. They're everywhere, and once you spot them, you see them all over. Is the sales pitch, persuasive argument, or editorial using statistics, emotion, anecdotes, or humor to make its point? As a side benefit, you learn to see through these tactics and spot the logic.

- » **Revisit your math.** Resist the urge to burn your geometry books the minute the semester is over. Keep your math notebooks and especially your old exams. Revisit the questions, especially the ones you missed, because these are the topics you'll see on the SAT. Research shows that memory improves when concepts are reviewed after a period of time, and this will help when the SAT asks you to factor a quadratic, which you may not have done for a couple of years.

- » **Take practice exams.** Work your way through all the questions and then check the answers and explanations to everything you got wrong, skipped, or wobbled on. After identifying areas of focus, you know where you have to practice. Block 4 of this book contains an abridged practice exam. You and find additional free practice exams at the College Board website: go to `https://satsuite.collegeboard.org/sat/practice-preparation`.

- » **Work on your writing.** Send a story in to the school newspaper or send letters or emails to a publication editor. Writing for an audience ups your writing game, because you pay much closer attention to your reasoning and grammar. Do this a few times, and you're a pro! This is especially true with the sort of questions that challenge your writing skills, because there are plenty of those that you have to answer correctly on the SAT.

- » **Download and practice with the Bluebook testing app.** This app is free to download from the College Board's website (`www.collegeboard.org`), and it's the best way to experience what the actual exam is like at a testing center or high school. Here you can take the digital SAT practice test and explore the online calculator, the reference screen with all the formulas, and the ability to annotate text and cross off wrong answers. Make sure you know how the app works. Don't discover these features on exam day — practice using them now.

- » **Check the device requirements.** As of this writing, you can take the digital SAT on your own laptop or tablet, provided it meets the requirements described on the College Board's website. If you don't have a device that meets these requirements, you can borrow one from your school — provided your school has one to spare.

Understanding Your Score

The SAT gives colleges an in-depth look at your skills and performance. If you take the exam more than once, as most students do, you can use the detailed information from your score reports to craft a personalized study program and zero in on the skills you need to fine-tune.

Composite score

Your exam score, called the *composite score*, is the score that everyone is worried about. It's the sum of the Reading and Writing section (200 to 800 points) and Math section (also 200 to 800 points). The maximum composite score is 1600, and the minimum is 400, which you get for showing up.

Score reports

At the time of this writing, the SAT provides four score reports, which can be sent to your choice of schools. (*Yikes?* Not really. More like, *Yes!*) If you want to send out more reports to more schools, you can do so for a nominal fee. Check the College Board website at `www.collegeboard.org` for current prices. You can request additional score reports when you sign up for the exam, when you take the exam, or after the fact. At the time of this writing, your scores are good for five years.

After you get your SAT scores, you can order a Question-and-Answer Service (QAS), which shows each question from the exam, which answer you selected, and if applicable, the correct answer. There may be a small fee for this, and the fee waiver may apply. If you are planning to retake the SAT, this service is a lifesaver: It's like turning on a light to see your exam performance. The bad thing is that this service isn't available for some tests, but the good thing is that it *is* available with your PSAT, so use that!

Score reports arrive in your mailbox and at your high school a few weeks after your test, and in your email about a week sooner. The College Board usually posts on its website the date that the test scores will be available.

Last thing. Be sure to create a free College Board account at www.collegeboard.org, where you can check your scores and register for the PSAT and SAT. Here, along with your score, you can find how well you did in comparison to everyone else who took the exam when you did. You can also immediately access the QAS and get right to the questions. Plus, you can get the Bluebook app and practice SAT pdfs, all for free.

Block 2
Reading and Writing Section

SAT Reading and Writing consists of 54 passages divided into two 27-question modules. Each passage has one to two paragraphs, graphs, or data sets, and a single question. You have 32 minutes per module for 64 minutes total. Here's what to expect on this test:

>> **Sentence Completion Questions:** Each question contains one to three sentences with a blank space indicating a missing word. Your task is to follow the logic of the text so that you can choose the best word to fill in the blank. Answering these questions depends on your knowledge of vocabulary and your ability to use the clues in the context of the sentence to find the best word to fill in the blank. There are about six or seven of these texts, with one question per passage.

>> **Critical Reading Questions:** Short excerpts from different content areas are followed by a question that tests your understanding of the writer's craft and structure and/or the information and ideas in the text. The excerpts are taken from literature (prose and poetry), social science, history, and natural science, and some questions may be based on a paired set of texts. These questions may ask you to compare, contrast, or synthesize ideas. Many texts are accompanied by graphs or charts. You may be asked to analyze data or synthesize information from text and a graphic.

>> **Standard English Convention Questions:** Paragraphs of one to three sentences measure your ability to edit text to conform to the conventions of Standard English. A single question after each passage tests your understanding of sentence structure, usage, and punctuation.

>> **Research and Graphics Questions:** Some passages, typically science but sometimes social studies, are based on charts, graphs, or diagrams (often, but not always, accompanied by text), like those that appear in textbooks.

Getting Up to Speed on Test-Taking Strategies

Scoring high on standardized tests goes beyond merely knowing the subject matter; it requires managing your time effectively, not allowing your anxiety to shake your confidence, and carefully and quickly analyzing answer choices. In this section, I reveal strategies for reading passages faster with better comprehension, analyzing answer choices and choosing the best answer fast, and putting the strategies into practice.

Reading faster with better comprehension

The biggest challenge in the Reading and Writing section of the SAT is answering all the questions before your time runs out. To meet this challenge, start with this simple step-by-step approach:

1. **Read the question first.** Each passage is followed by a single question; read the question first so you know what to look for in the passage. For example, if the question asks about Standard English conventions, you know to read the passage and pay attention to the grammar. If the question is on critical thinking, you know to pay attention to the passage's logic.

TIP

Look for keywords in the question. Whether the question asks for the writer's main point or purpose, or the choice that *weakens* or *counters* the writer's claim, this clues you in to what to look for in the passage.

2. **Read the passage.**

Armed with what the question tells you to look for, you can skim or delve deep into the passage looking for clues. The Bluebook app (mentioned in Block 1) allows you to highlight and annotate text, so practice using these features with the app.

3. **Save the time-intensive questions for last.**

Each question in the module is worth the same points, whether you answer it in one minute or five. You don't want to work through the time-intensive questions and then run out of time before reaching the questions you can answer quickly! If the question looks like it's too time-consuming, mark it for review and come back to it after answering the other questions. Most students are faster with the Standard English convention questions, but use practice tests to evaluate your strengths.

TIP

The Bluebook app has a built-in timer, so keep track of how much time you've used and how much time you have left. With 32 minutes per module, you should be halfway through the module (about question 14) at the 16-minute mark.

4. **Follow the one-minute-per-question rule.**

Imagine this. You take five minutes to answer a tough question, you get it right (which you find out later), and then you run out of time before reaching the last three questions of the module! Who won: you or that tough question?

I'd say the question won, so don't make that mistake. Instead, if you're stuck on a question, skip it and come back to it later. Follow these steps:

1. **Guess an answer.** If time expires before you return to this question, at least you threw a mental dart for a 25 percent chance of getting it right.

2. **Mark the question for review.** This way, of course, you know which question to return to.

REMEMBER

If you want to return to a question, click Mark for Review right on the screen, above the question. Then you can check the Review screen from anywhere in the module to see a list of questions you've marked for review or you have left to answer.

Don't mark for review every question that you have any doubt on! When you have five minutes remaining, and the review screen shows 20 questions marked for review, you have no idea which answers are probably right and which ones are complete guesses that you need to return to. Instead, mark the question for review *only* if you make a guess.

3. **Go on to the next question.** Follow the one-minute-per-question rule and complete the module.

    If you end up not returning to the question marked for review, at least you (maybe) lost only one point, which is better than losing the handful of points at the end of the module.

Almost no one gets a perfect score. Your job isn't to answer *all* the questions correctly: It's to answer *more* questions correctly than most of the other test-takers. If you missed a question, they probably also missed that question.

Finding the right answer fast

It's all about the strategies, right? With 32 minutes to answer 27 questions per module, you have slightly over a minute per question. All you need to do is find the right answer or eliminate all the wrong answers. Here's a strategy for accelerating your ability to narrow your choices and identify the correct answer:

1. **Cover the answer choices.**

    Place your hand or scratch paper on the screen to cover the answers. Seems silly, right? But this way, you're not tempted to glance at the answers. Sure, the right answer is there, but three trap answers are also there. Dodge these traps and ***focus on the question.***

2. **Answer the question yourself.**

    After reading the question and the passage, answer the question in your own words, *without* looking at the answer choices.

3. **Cross off the wrong answers.**

    Your answer won't match the right answer. It doesn't have to. What it *will* do is make three answer choices appear so far out in left field that they couldn't possibly be correct. Here's what you do:

    (a) **Move your hand or paper down just a little to show Choice (A).**

    You're covering the answers, remember? Now show just the first answer. Based on your own answer, could this be right? That answer is hardly ever *yes*. More often it's either *not a chance* or *I'm not sure*. If it's *not a chance*, use the software to cross it off. If it's *I'm not sure*, leave it. **Don't spend time on it.** Either cross it off or leave it and *move on*.

    (b) **Move your hand or paper down a little more to show Choice (B).**

    Here's the thing. Sometimes an answer is so clearly, impossibly wrong that you can cross it off as soon as you read it. If you're not sure, leave it. Either way, move *quickly* to either cross off or leave each answer choice.

    (c) **Repeat the process with Choices (C) and (D).**

    One at a time, either cross off or leave each answer. Typically, you'll have three crossed off and one remaining, so go with the remaining answer and get to the next question. If you have two answer choices remaining, check them to see which is more likely. If you can't tell, that's okay: Take a guess, mark the question for review, and *move on*.

When does this strategy fail? When you go straight for the answer choices without thinking of your own answer first. What happens is that you get caught in the trap of wrong answers, where you read each answer and think, "Maybe *that's* it" and spend valuable time going back and forth to the passage. Don't do that!

Also, don't doubt your own answer when you read the answer choices. Sure, the correct answer may contain more depth and detail than your answer — but so may the three wrong answers. Trust yourself to answer the question well enough! No matter how far off your own answer is, it'll be good enough for you to eliminate three wrong answers.

No one gets a perfect score on SAT Reading and Writing, so don't kill yourself trying to. It's okay to miss a question here and there — but it's not okay to spend five minutes on one question and then run out of time leaving a bunch of questions unanswered.

Putting the strategies to use

Strategies take practice. You're not used to them, and it's easy to mess up the first few times. That's okay. Practice the strategies, get them wrong, forget certain steps — *before* exam day. That's what practice is for.

Practice questions

This excerpt is from the science text, *The Dancing Mouse: A Study in Animal Behavior*, by Robert M. Yerkes.

> As a rule the dancing mouse is considerably smaller than the common mouse. All the dancing mice had black eyes and were smaller as well as weaker than the common gray house mouse. The weakness, indicated by their inability to hold up their own weight or to cling to an object, curiously enough does not manifest itself in their dancing; in this they are tireless. Frequently they run in circles or whirl about with astonishing rapidity for several minutes at a time.

Line

(05)

The detail question

Detail questions are often *keyword* questions, where you look back in the text for keywords from the question.

For example: Which choice best states an unexpected quality of the dancing mouse?

Cover the answer choices! Think about the detail in the passage that was surprising or unexpected.

(A) The dancing mouse is smaller and weaker than the common mouse.

(B) The dancing mouse has black eyes.

(C) The dancing mouse can dance energetically.

(D) The dancing mouse cannot cling to an object.

How did you do? Did you cross off Choices (A), (B), and (D)?

(A)	Smaller and weaker	Cross this off: True, but nothing in the text indicates that this is unexpected.
(B)	Black eyes	Cross this off: True, but nothing in the text indicates that this is unexpected.
(C)	Dance energetically	Place a dot: The text states that the weakness of the dancing mouse does not **curiously** carry over into its dancing.
(D)	Cling to an object	Cross this off: True, but nothing in the text indicates that this is unexpected.

While the descriptions in Choices (A), (B), and (D) are true statements about the dancing mice, nothing in the text indicates these characteristics are surprising. But the text states that *curiously*, the weakness of the dancing mice does not extend to their dancing. The word *curiously* is your clue that Choice (C) presents something unexpected about the dancing mouse.

Continuing with the detail questions

Here's another example where you focus on a keyword.

PLAY

According to the text, in what way does the dancing mouse not have a weakness?

Cover the answers. In what way do *you* think the dancing mouse is superior? (Never mind how that sounds.) Reread the paragraph and focus on the mouse's abilities. Skim the passage for the keyword "weakness."

It seems that the mouse only has weaknesses, but it's *tireless* in dancing. Keep that in mind now, and cross off the wrong answers:

(A) endurance

(B) muscle strength

(C) visual acuity

(D) tenacity

Did you cross off Choices (B), (C), and (D)? They're so impossible that it *has* to be Choice (A). Here's the process:

(A)	Endurance	Place a dot: "Endurance" is in the ballpark of "tireless."
(B)	Muscle strength	Cross this off: It has nothing to do with "tireless."
(C)	Visual acuity	Cross this off: It's not even close (though the passage mentions the mouse's eyes, don't misinterpret this).
(D)	Tenacity	Cross this off: *Tenacity* means "ability to cling," and though it may relate to "tireless," the passage refers to dancing, not clinging.

WARNING

The word "tireless" by itself could match "tenacity," like when you're clinging to the handles of a jet ski. Be sure to keep the context in mind when checking the answer choices.

Inference and main idea questions

An *inference* is a conclusion that you reach based on evidence, and SAT Reading and Writing has many of these questions. You get a certain amount of information, and then you have to stretch it a little. The questions may resemble the following:

>> The author implies which of the following about college admissions success and using *Digital SAT 5-Hour Quick Prep For Dummies?*

>> Which of the following statements would the author most likely agree with regarding college and career path?

Inference questions require a certain amount of reading between the lines and thinking about what the writer implies. Read the passage and do what you did before: Cover the answer choices, answer the question yourself, and cross off wrong answers.

Try this inference question, based on these sentences about the westward journey of settlers during the 19th century.

PLAY

During the arduous cross-country trek, the women generally do the driving, while the men and boys bring up the rear with horses and cattle of all grades, from poor, weak calves to fine, fat animals, that show they have had a good living where they came from.

Line

With which statement would the travelers described in this passage probably agree?

Cover the answers! Of course, you can't predict "which one," but you *can* think of what the answer *could* be. What do *you* think the travelers' attitude would be like? How about, "The women are sick of driving and the men are sick of handling animals."

Now: Cross off wrong answers.

(A) Only healthy animals can survive a long journey.

(B) All livestock should be treated equally.

(C) Gender distinctions are considerations in assigning work.

(D) Many pioneers are motivated by greed.

Did you cross off Choices (A), (B), and (D)? They're so impossible that it *must be* Choice (C). Here's the detail:

(A)	Only healthy animals can survive a long journey.	Cross this off.
(B)	All livestock should be treated equally.	Cross this off.
(C)	Gender distinctions are considerations in assigning work.	Maybe. The men handled animals and the women drove. Leave this one.
(D)	Many pioneers are motivated by greed.	This may be true, but it doesn't match your answer and it's not supported by anything in the passage.

Now for a main idea question from the same short passage.

PLAY

Which of the following is closest to the main idea of the passage?

Cover those answers. What do *you* think the main idea is? Something like, "The settlers had a difficult journey west." Keep it simple.

Now cross off wrong answers:

(A) The cattle varied in quality.

(B) The westward journey was slow and difficult.

(C) Horses brought up the rear.

(D) Women were better drivers even then.

Did you cross off Choices (A), (C), and (D)? They're so far from your answer that it *must be* Choice (B). Here's why:

(A)	The cattle varied in quality.	Cross this off: It may be true, but it's not the main idea, and it doesn't match your answer.
(B)	The westward journey was slow and difficult.	Leave this one: It's not far from your answer.
(C)	Horses brought up the rear.	Cross this off: Also true, but it's not the main idea, and it also doesn't match your answer.
(D)	Women were better drivers even then.	Cross this off: It might be true through the ages, but it doesn't match your answer.

Note a pattern in these main idea answer choices: Even the wrong answers may be true and/or stated somewhere in the passage, but being true or stated doesn't make it the *main idea*.

Main purpose questions

Main purpose questions ask you to figure out what the writer is trying to accomplish in the passage. Writers write for so many different reasons. Does the passage make a claim? Support or refute a point of view? Challenge an idea that is accepted by others? Offer a new interpretation? Your task is to determine why the writer wrote this passage.

PLAY

To cite the old proverb, "We live in interesting times." One indicator: just pause from reading this book for a moment and reflect on the recently invented digital devices you have close at hand. Open up your smartphone or tablet and observe a cornucopia of entertainment and lifestyle apps — games, photography, music, cooking, sports — as well as social media and messaging apps that link you to friends, family, and colleagues across the globe, anytime. Most of us have instant access to the world's information via powerful, personalized search engines that fit in our pockets. Later in the book we talk to experts who now wonder about the burdens of being always connected. But how often have you wondered, "How on Earth did we live without our devices?"

Line

(05)

Which choice best states the writer's purpose in including the proverb?

(A) To place attention on how interesting modern devices can be

(B) To show the foresight held by old wisdom

(C) To remind the reader that things have always been changing

(D) To reflect on how things today are so different

Cover the answers. In your own words, describe why you think the author quotes an old proverb in a passage about new electronics? Possibly the writer wants the reader to think about the idea that the more things change, the more they stay the same, reminding the reader that in life, things are always changing.

Now, thinking about your answer, cross off wrong choices. Did you cross off Choices (A), (B), and (D)? You're left with Choice (C), which is close to your own answer.

Focusing on Specific Content Areas

SAT Reading passages come in three basic flavors: Literature, Social Studies, and Science. The Literature passages include excerpts from prose (short stories, novels, essays) and poetry. These passages aren't in any particular order, so you may have to switch gears from poetry to science just like that.

Social studies

If the passage is about social studies (history, anthropology, sociology, education, cultural studies, and so on), keep these tips in mind when you read the whole passage:

>> **Go for the positive.** The SAT doesn't criticize anyone with the power to sue or contact the media. So, if you see a question about the author's tone or viewpoint, look for a positive spin.

>> **Note the structure.** The passage frequently presents a claim and supports it with facts, statistics, or quotations from experts. If you're asked about the significance of a particular detail in a passage, the detail is probably evidence in the case that the author is making.

>> **Identify cause and effect.** History and social studies passages often explain *why* something happens. Search for keywords such as *therefore, hence, consequently,* and others that signal a reason.

>> **Look for opposing ideas.** Experts, including historians, are into criticizing each other's interpretations of archaeological discoveries or important events. (Maybe they do this to assert themselves, but anyway . . .) Some social studies passages may present two or more viewpoints, especially in the two-part passages. Look for the opposing sides or find the main theory and the objections to it.

To put these tips into action, here is a brief history passage taken from *To and Through Nebraska*, by Frances I. Sims Fulton, describing settlers traveling to the West during the 19th century.

PLAY

During all this time, and despite the disagreeable weather, emigrants from the cities of the Northeast to the wilderness in the West keep up the line of march, traveling in their "prairie schooners," as the great hoop-covered wagon is called, into which, often are packed their every worldly possession, and have room to pile in a large family on top. Sometimes a sheet-iron stove is carried along at the rear of the wagon, which, when needed, they set up inside and put the pipe through a hole in the covering. Those who do not have this convenience carry wood with them and build a fire on the ground to cook by; cooking utensils are generally packed in a box at the side or front. The coverings of the wagons are of all shades and materials. When oil cloth is not used, they are often patched over the top with their oil-cloth table covers, saving them from the rain.

Line

(05)

(10)

Which choice best states the purpose of the details about the wagon?

Cover the answers. In your own words, why does the author describe the covered wagons in so much detail? Probably to give an example of how the travelers are resourceful and clever. Now cross off wrong answers:

(A) Reveal the convenience of covered wagons.

(B) Emphasize the ingenuity of the travelers.

(C) Show that the travelers were ill-equipped for life on the frontier.

(D) Contrast life in the city with life in the wilderness.

Did you cross off Choices (A), (C), and (D), leaving Choice (B) as the only possible answer? Here's the rationale. According to the passage, the travelers pack everything they need into one wagon. Some have more than others, but those who, for example, lack stoves "carry wood with them and build a fire on the ground." They protect themselves from the rain with either a wagon cover or a tablecloth.

PLAY

Which of the following best fits the theme of this passage?

Cover the answers. In your own words, what's the passage mainly about? Maybe something like, "Traveling and camping in a covered wagon." Perfect. Now cross off those wrong answers:

(A) Cooking on the frontier

(B) Chasing the gold rush

(C) Traveling in a prairie schooner

(D) Economics of the Old West

Cross off Choice (A), because even though cooking is part of it, it's not the main idea. Cross off Choice (B) which, though it may be true, isn't specific enough to be the correct answer, and more importantly, doesn't match your answer. Choice (C) stays: Remember that "prairie schooner" is what they called the covered wagons. Cross off Choice (D), which isn't even mentioned in the passage. Choice (C) is left, so that's what you go with.

Science

Science passages don't rely on your knowledge of the topic: Everything you need to know to answer the questions is in the passages. You are expected to know the basics — for example, the Earth orbits the Sun, water boils when it's heated, cells divide — but there's no need to study the science topics to prepare for these passages. Instead, practice the strategies.

These passages cover such science topics as biology, chemistry, environmental science, physics, experiments, and various phenomena. Try this approach when reading a science passage:

>> **Search out the facts.** Whether describing an experiment, survey, or observation, all the information you need to know is in the text or in the graphic element. Pay attention to numbers, including percentages, populations, and rates of growth or change.

>> **Don't worry about technical terms, but do know general science vocabulary.** If you see a strange word, the definition is probably tucked into the sentence. You won't encounter a question based on the definition of *Tephritidae* unless the passage explains what it is. (It's a type of fruit fly.) You should, however, know general terms that pop up frequently in science-related material, such as *control group* (a group that doesn't participate in an experiment and serves as a point of comparison) and *catalyst* (something that causes or increases the rate of change, as in a chemical process). As you work through practice exams, jot down these general terms from the answer explanations, because you may see them again on exam day.

>> **Identify the argument.** Some SAT science passages present a dispute between two viewpoints. The question may zero in on the evidence for each scientific theory or hypothesis, and then quiz you about each author's stance.

>> **Notice the examples.** The SAT science passages tend to offer examples both in the text and in the graphics. The questions may ask what the examples prove.

If the question includes a graphic element, like a chart, then follow these guidelines:

- » **Look at everything.** The title; the explanation on the top, bottom, or sides; the labels inside a diagram — *everything*. Don't memorize it, but notice it: Is there a pattern or contrast? Are the numbers on the side in thousands? If a graph reaches the level of 12, you need to know whether this represents 12 actual or 12 thousand.

- » **Note the variables.** The *variable* is the part that changes. Some graphs include more than one — perhaps a solid line showing peanut butter sales and a dotted line tracing jelly sales.

- » **Note the relationship between the graphic and the text.** Usually, these work together. A bar graph may tell you how many test-takers earned scholarships, while the text may explain how one scholarship freed up funds for a Jeep. It could happen. Anyway, together these statistics paint a clear picture.

Try this visual-elements question:

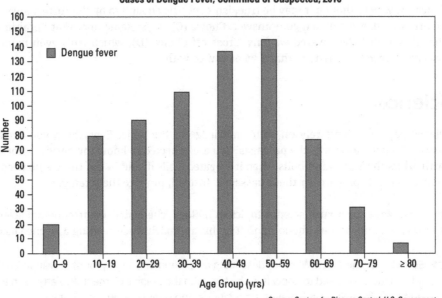

Cases of Dengue Fever, Confirmed or Suspected, 2010

Source: Centers for Disease Control, U.S. Government

PLAY

The information in the passage supports which statement about Dengue fever?

Cover the answers. In your own words, what do you think is up with the fever? It seems to hit middle-aged folks the hardest. Good thing you're young. Anyway, with this middle-aged point in mind, cross off the wrong answers:

(A) Infants are less likely to contract Dengue fever than the elderly.

(B) In 2010, most cases of Dengue fever occurred in people aged 40 to 60.

(C) The risk of catching Dengue fever rises with age.

(D) Dengue fever is especially dangerous for infants and children.

Choices (A), (C), and (D) are easy targets to cross off, leaving Choice (B) as the only possible answer. This is because the bars for ages 40 to 49 and 50 to 59 are higher than those for other age groups.

Literature

Questions on literature may ask you to read part of a poem or story and interpret the lines, understand a character's motivations, understand the theme, describe the structure of a text, or indicate the function of a selected line from the text.

Keep these tips in mind:

>> **Look for the big picture.** Ask yourself, "What do I know about what's going on in this poem or story?" Things may be symbolic or representative, or they might stand out in the author's narrative for a reason. For example, something like, "Joan never forgot seeing the keys on the table." What's important about those keys? Pay attention to how this detail in the story reveals something about Joan's character.

>> **Stay attuned to word choice.** A literature passage is perfectly suited to questions about the author's tone (*bitter, nostalgic, fond, critical*, and so forth). Pay attention to the feelings associated with certain words.

>> **Visualize the narrative.** Read the paragraph as if you're watching a scene from a movie. This will help you understand the nuances and symbolism that fuel many of the literature passage questions.

Try this question, based on an excerpt from *Kew Gardens*, a story by Virginia Woolf. Visualize the narrative and look for the symbolism:

PLAY

"Fifteen years ago I came here with Lily," he thought. "We sat somewhere over there by a lake and I begged her to marry me all through the hot afternoon. How the dragonfly kept circling round us: how clearly I see the dragonfly and her shoe with the square silver buckle at the toe. All the time I spoke I saw her shoe and when it moved impatiently I knew without looking up what she was going to say: the whole of her seemed to be in her shoe. And my love, my desire, were in the dragonfly; for some reason I thought that if it settled there, on that leaf, she would say "Yes" at once. But the dragonfly went round and round: it never settled anywhere — of course not, happily not, or I shouldn't be walking here with Eleanor and the children."

Line

(05)

In this passage, the speaker's attitude may best be characterized as _____.

Cover the answers. What do you think characterizes the speaker's attitude? Maybe something like, desperate for the dragonfly to make Lily say yes, but then glad it didn't? Now cross off the wrong answers:

(A) mocking

(B) confused

(C) nostalgic

(D) argumentative

Desperate and *glad* don't connect with Choices (A), (B), or (D), so cross those right off, leaving Choice (C) as the only possible answer. And it's right. Here's why: In this paragraph, the speaker looks at the past, remembering an afternoon when he "begged" Lily to accept his marriage proposal. He's feeling pleasure and sadness at remembering the past, which of course is *nostalgic*, Choice (C). The sadness shows in Lily's refusal, which he now sees "happily." Choice (B), *confused*, doesn't match because he wasn't confused: He simply changed his mind, and apparently dodged a bullet.

And, of course, SAT Literature loves symbolism. Try this one:

PLAY

In this passage, Lily's shoe most likely represents _____.

Cover the answers. What do *you* think her shoe represents? Maybe a counterpart to the dragonfly that will not cooperate and also Lily's feelings. Something like that. Your answer doesn't have to be close. It just has to be something that you think of without looking at the answers. Now cross off wrong ones.

(A) Lily's desire to protect others

(B) Lily's reluctance to settle down

(C) Lily's love for the narrator

(D) the narrator's attraction to Lily

See? When you think of your own answer, even if it's far out there, it makes the wrong answers *really easy* to cross off. You should have easily crossed off Choices (A), (C), and (D), leaving Choice (B), though iffy, as the only possible answer, and the right one. *That* is how you turn a challenging question into an easy one.

TIP

The answer that you think of hardly ever matches the right answer exactly. That's okay — *it doesn't have to.* Your self-thought answer serves a much more important role: *It makes the wrong answers stand out like weeds in a garden.* Cross 'em off, go with the remaining one, and that's all you have time to do in the roughly one-minute-per-question that you get in the Reading and Writing section.

Poetry

Reading poetry (verse) is a little different from reading prose (sentences and paragraphs). Poetry is written in lines, typically in a *cadence* (rhythm), and it may have unusual *syntax* (word order).

On the SAT you may read short poems or excerpts from longer poems. Be sure to review any introductory information, as it provides helpful context to the poem.

Try this one:

PLAY

The following poem was written by British poet William Wordsworth in 1802.

My Heart Leaps Up When I Behold

My heart leaps up when I behold

A rainbow in the sky:

So was it when my life began;

So is it now I am a man;

So be it when I shall grow old,

Or let me die!

The Child is father of the Man;

And I could wish my days to be

Bound each to each by natural piety.

Which choice best describes the overall structure of the text?

Cover the answers. How would you describe the structure of the text? The speaker sees a rainbow that makes him happy always and forever (now, as a boy, still as an old man). Your answer doesn't have to be perfect: It just has to be close.

Now cross off wrong answers.

(A) The writer examines an occurrence in nature and realizes it's a sign that his life is almost over.

(B) The writer first examines his outer life and then compares that insight to his inner life.

(C) The writer finds joy in a natural phenomenon and traces that response through three time periods in his life.

(D) The writer sees a natural phenomenon and then questions its role in his life.

Choice (A) goes: The writer doesn't think the rainbow is a sign that his life is over.

Choice (B) goes: The writer doesn't compare his outer life to his inner life.

Choice (C) stays: The writer finds joy in the rainbow and connects it to phases in his life.

Choice (D) goes: The writer doesn't question the role of the rainbow in his life.

And the correct answer is Choice (C). But you already knew that.

See how this works? When you think of your own answer, even if it's not even nearly anywhere close to the correct answer, it still does its job by making the wrong answers *easier* to cross off. *That* is how you turn a challenging question into an easy one.

Tackling English Vocabulary and Conventions Questions

Now, start fine-tuning the strategies covered in the previous section. Stick with the one-minute-per-question rule and remember: Almost no one gets a perfect SAT score, but as long as your score is higher than the scores of most other SAT-takers (which it will be, because you're using this book, and they're not), you'll do well enough to reach or exceed your goals in college admissions.

Becoming sentence completion and in-context vocabulary savvy

To answer these questions, consider the context of the narrative, and pay attention to the word's definition and *connotation* (feeling and associations in addition to literal meaning). Try this one:

PLAY

The U.S. Fish and Wildlife Service warns campers, hikers, and hunters to avoid encounters with bears. In any encounter with a bear in the wild, the behavior of the human matters. If a bear is rummaging through a trash can and takes little notice of you, then slowly leave the area and move to a safer location. If the bear appears to be more curious or aggressive and approaches, stand your ground and be prepared to use bear spray. The bear's behavior should _____ your response.

(A) ignore

(B) mimic

(C) determine

(D) follow

Now for the strategy.

> **First:** Cover the answer choices and fill in the blank yourself. Consider the context clues in the sentence. The text states that *in encounters with a bear, the behavior of the human matters.*
>
> **Next:** Think logically. If you take different actions depending on what the bear does, then the bear's behavior should let you know what you should do.
>
> **Now:** Think of the word that you would use to fill in the blank, without looking at the choices (because they're covered up, right?). You probably came up with a word like "cause." Now that you have your answer, cross off the wrong answer choices.

Choice (A) is out, as you can't rely on the bear to ignore your response. Cross it off.

Choice (B) isn't very logical, so cross it off.

Choice (C) makes sense. If your response depends on the bear's behavior, then the bear's behavior should determine (or cause) your response. Leave it.

Choice (D) doesn't work as you can't count on the bear to follow your actions. Cross it off.

The remaining answer is the correct answer, Choice (C).

Nice. Now for some more.

PLAY

Images from the Hubble Space Telescope reveal a small galaxy labeled UGCA 307. It consists of a diffuse band of stars containing red bubbles of gas that mark regions of recent star formations. Appearing as just a small patch of stars, UGCA 307 is a diminutive dwarf galaxy without a _____ structure, resembling nothing more than a hazy patch of passing cloud.

(A) blurry

(B) brittle

(C) heavy

(D) defined

Use the strategy: Cover the answer choices, read the sentence, and focus on the context clues. It's important to remember you are looking for a word that describes what the structure of the galaxy is *without*. What do you know about the structure of UGCA 307?

>> It's a small galaxy.

>> It appears as a patch of stars.

>> It resembles a hazy patch of passing cloud.

So, what kind of structure is UGCA 307 without or lacking? If the galaxy resembles a hazy patch, then it is without a clear shape or a sharp outline.

Now check the answers.

(A) blurry: That is what it does look like, so it wouldn't be without a blurry structure. Cross it out.

(B) brittle: There's nothing in the text about soft or brittle, so brittle doesn't make sense. Cross it out.

(C) heavy: Again, nothing in the text about weight. Cross it out.

(D) defined: Having a defined structure is the opposite of having a hazy shape, so leave this one.

Choice (D) remains, so go with that.

The correct answer is Choice (D).

Now for another:

PLAY

Raj was _____ about performing in the student talent show. Although he was pleased and honored about being chosen, he was very nervous about performing before such a large audience of his classmates, friends, and family.

(A) cheerful

(B) proud

(C) fearful

(D) ambivalent

You have several context clues in this sentence, but they seem to contradict each other:

>> Raj was pleased.

>> Raj was honored.

>> Raj was very nervous.

The missing word obviously describes Raj, so how does he feel? Seems he's both pleased and nervous, so your answer is something like *mixed up*, *confused*, or *unsure*.

Now cross off wrong answers.

(A) cheerful: Yes, but he's also nervous. Cross it out.

(B) proud: Yes, but he's also fearful. Cross it out.

(C) fearful: Yes, but he's also pleased and honored. Cross it out.

(D) ambivalent. If you don't know this word, the prefix *ambi-* means "both" (like *ambidextrous* — two-handed), and Raj feels both pleased and nervous. *Ambivalent* means having mixed or contradictory feelings and is the perfect word to fit in the blank.

The correct answer is Choice (D).

As you enhance your SAT prep by reading college-level publications (you *are* doing this, aren't you?), do a quick look-up of any unfamiliar word and jot down (or just think of) what it means. This is easy enough. If you're reading online, right-click or tap the word; if you're reading print, you can actually say, "Okay Google (or Siri, or Alexa), define *nomenclature*."

Reviewing grammar, punctuation, and usage

The conventions of Standard English questions cover the basic rules of grammar, punctuation, usage, and rhetoric that you're expected to know in college. On these questions, you'll see a blank space in a text that you have to fill in with a choice that best completes the sentence according to the conventions of Standard English. Here are some topics to get you started:

>> **Incorrect punctuation:** Apostrophes and commas may be extra, missing, or in the wrong place. The SAT also mixes up colons and semicolons for you to sort out.

>> **Incomplete sentences:** *Run-ons* (sentences with two subjects and two verbs) must be properly joined, and *fragments* (such as a sentence with a subject but no verb — for example, "The dog.") must be completed.

>> **Misplaced modifiers:** A *modifier* (adjective or adverb) must be near the word that it modifies. For example, this is incorrect: "The skier went off the trail, laughing loudly." *Laughing loudly* is the modifier, so it should be near *the skier*, not *the trail*; otherwise, the sentence reads as if the *trail* were laughing. Maybe it was.

>> **Wrong homophones:** Do you turn right or turn write? Is the tree taller than or taller then the tent? English has many homophones, but the SAT just asks about the common ones.

>> **Wrong verb tense:** Make sure the verb tense expresses the right time for an event or state of being or your answer you choose *was* wrong . . . I mean *will be* wrong.

>> **Lack of subject-verb agreement:** In a sentence, the verb must match the subject in number, person, and gender, so "The butterflies flutters through the air" is wrong because *butterflies* is a plural noun and *flutters* is the singular form of the verb.

>> **Parallel structure:** Parallelism requires that items in a series be similar in length and grammatical form; for example, in the sentence "The dog runs, jumps, and pants," all three verbs in the series are one word and all in the same form. In contrast, in the sentence "The dog runs, jumps, and stole the steak right off my plate," the final verb is a multi-word phrase and is in a different tense. It's not always that obvious.

Besides what *to* look for, here's what *not* to look for. This is the Don't Worry list:

>> **Don't worry about spelling.** The SAT doesn't test spelling except for those homophones.

>> **Don't worry about capitalization.** The SAT very infrequently takes on capitalization. Assume that a word is capitalized properly unless a glaring mistake jumps out at you.

REMEMBER

When you answer the conventions of Standard English questions, be sure that your answer choice completes the sentence without any grammatical error. You must be able to place the answer choice in the blank and end up with a properly worded result.

Ready to practice? Try this sample question.

PLAY

The water beyond the mangrove trees _____ including tires, chunks of wood, and plastic trash bags.

(A) were not only polluted but also laden with debris

(B) not only polluted but were also laden with debris

(C) not only polluted but also debris was laden there

(D) was not only polluted but also laden with debris

This sentence has one subject, *the water,* paired with two predicates, *was polluted* and *laden with debris.* The verb *was* is missing from *laden with debris.* Choice (A) uses the plural verb *were* instead of the singular verb *was* to agree with water, so cross it off. Choices (B) and (C) remove *was* from *polluted,* among other errors, so cross them off as well. Choice (D) places *was* before *not only,* so *was* applies to both predicates, and is the correct answer.

TIP

For a full-scale grammar refresher, take a look at the latest editions of *English Grammar For Dummies* and *English Grammar Workbook For Dummies* (both authored by Geraldine Woods and published by Wiley).

Continuing with transitions

A *transition* establishes the relationship between two clauses, which are usually a series of events. The question asks you to pick the transition that makes the most sense. For example, you wouldn't say, "She got in her car *because* she drove away" or "She got in her car and *however* drove away." You would say, "She got in her car and *then* drove away."

Here are some common transitions that you'll find on the SAT.

>> **Contrast:** "He loves ice cream, *but* he hates Rocky Road." Other contrast words include *however, although, otherwise, on the other hand,* and *never/nonetheless.*

>> **Joining:** "She loves music, *and* she loves the blues." Other joining words include *moreover, further, likewise, in addition,* and *besides.*

>> **A results in B:** "He watered the plants, *so* they grew tall." Other "A results in B" words include *therefore, afterwards,* and *consequently.*

>> **B results in A:** "The car was clean *after* she washed it." Other "B results in A" words are *because* and *since.*

Don't try to memorize these, but rather learn to recognize them and use logic to understand the relationships they establish in the sentence. That's easier and more useful. Try it out on this practice question:

PLAY

The sequoia, a type of redwood, is the largest species of tree in the world, growing as tall as 280 feet. _____ sequoia trunks remain wide high up — for example, 60 feet above their base. General Sherman, the tallest living sequoia, is 17.5 feet wide.

(A) Furthermore,

(B) Otherwise,

(C) Therefore,

(D) However,

The fact that sequoias remain wide high up is a characteristic of this type of tree, so out go Choices (B) and (D). The fact that the tree is the tallest doesn't necessarily mean it will be wide at the top, so cross off Choice (C). The only answer left is Choice (A), *furthermore,* which is a *joining* transition, and the phrase that follows it provides an additional detail about the species.

Verb matching

Verb matching includes singular to singular, plural to plural, and consistent verb tense. In terms of agreement, the SAT asks about:

>> Subject-verb pairs

>> Pronoun-antecedent pairs

SUBJECT-VERB AGREEMENT

A *verb* expresses action or state of being; the *subject* is whoever or whatever is *doing* the action or *in* the state of being. A singular subject takes a singular verb, and a plural subject takes a plural verb. Check out these examples:

>> "The *snowmobiler chases* James Bond." *Snowmobiler* is a singular subject; *chases* is a singular verb.

>> "Six more *snowmobilers join* the pursuit." *Snowmobilers* is a plural subject; *join* is a plural verb.

The SAT expands upon this with trickier arrangements, like these:

>> ***There/here.*** These words aren't subjects. The subject comes *after* the verb, like this:

"Here are three calculators." The subject is *calculators,* matching the verb *are.*

>> ***Either/or*** and ***neither/nor.*** These words may join two subjects, so match the verb to the closest subject:

● "Neither the car nor the *tires are* in the garage." *Tires* is the closest subject, so the plural verb *are* is correct.

● "Neither the tools nor the *truck is* in the shop." *Truck* is the closest subject, so the singular verb *is* is correct.

>> **Interrupters between the subject-verb pair.** If an interrupter, such as a modifier or prepositional phrase, comes between the subject and the verb, it doesn't change the verb form.

This is correct: "The soda machine, along with the games, *is* perfect for the basement." *Along with the games* is an interrupter, so the singular subject *soda machine* stays with the singular verb *is.* An interrupter could also be set off by dashes: "The dog — after chasing the cats — is chasing a car."

REMEMBER

Two singular nouns joined by *and* make a plural. For example, "The fox and the hound *are* both inside." *The fox* and *the hound* together make a plural subject.

NOUN-PRONOUN AGREEMENT

The noun that the pronoun refers to is called an *antecedent.* Regardless of what it's called, it's the word that a pronoun replaces. In the sentence, "The receiver chased the ball and caught it," *it* is a pronoun, and *the ball* is the antecedent because *it* stands for *the ball.* The rule on antecedents is simple: Singular goes with singular and plural goes with plural. You probably already know all the easy applications of this rule. In the *receiver/ball* sentence, you'd never dream of replacing *the ball* with *them.* The SAT-makers, however, go for the tricky combinations:

>> **Pronouns containing _one, thing,_ or _body_ are singular.** Match these pronouns with other singular pronouns.

"Everyone brought *his or her* cheat sheet." *Everyone* is singular because it has *one* in it, and it goes with the singular *his or her.* Same with *none* and *nobody.*

>> *Either, neither, each,* **and** *every* **are singular.** These words are sometimes followed by phrases that sound plural (*either of the boys* or *each father and son*), but these words are always singular.

"Neither of the boys brought *his* calculator." *Neither* is singular, so it goes with *his,* also singular.

WARNING

Watch out for traps based on recent changes in language. You may hear (or say) something like, "*Someone* is at the door, so let *them* in." However, *someone,* which is singular, doesn't go with *them,* which is plural, so on the SAT this would be wrong, even though in some forms of writing, this may be considered correct.

Easing verb tension

In the SAT Reading and Writing section, *tense* isn't just how you feel on the exam. It's the verb quality that indicates relative time. Remember these rules:

>> **The helping verbs** *has* **and** *have* **connect present and past actions.** When you see these helping verbs, something started in the past and is either still going on or just stopped. ("Rodney *has been* playing soccer all afternoon, and Julie *had been* watching until her phone rang.")

>> **The helping verb** *had* **places one past action before another past action.** ("Josephine *had scored* a goal before Rodney scored.")

>> **The tense doesn't change for the same subject.** You may see a sentence where the verbs change tense. "Charise *is cooking* dinner and *watches* TV," should be, "*watching* TV." If the second verb has a different tense, it needs a new subject.

TIP

A verb can also be contrary to the fact. This just means that when a statement isn't true, it's worded differently. (*If I were creating* the SAT, I would dump all the grammar questions. *If I had known* about the grammar questions, I wouldn't have thrown my English textbooks into the pool.) The *if* part of the sentence — the untrue part — gets *were* or *had,* and the other part of the sentence features *would.* The SAT-makers may place *if I would* or *if I was* to trip you up. Your job, of course, is to catch that and mark *if I were.*

Parallel writing

A favorite SAT question concerns *parallelism,* the way a sentence keeps its balance. The basic premise is simple: Each item in a series must be comparable in length and form. You can't "surf and soak up sun and playing in the sand" because *playing* is a different tense. You can "surf and soak up sun and play in the sand" without any problems — well, without any grammatical problems. Keep these pointers in mind:

>> **Look for lists.** Whenever you have a series of two or more items, be sure their wording is consistent. For example, in the sentence "The three qualities we value in our employees are honesty, integrity, and being creative," the last item in the series isn't parallel with the other three. Parallel structure would be "The three qualities we value in our employees are honesty, integrity, and creativity."

>> **Look for paired conjunctions.** Conjunctions are joining words. Three common paired conjunctions are *either/or*, *neither/nor*, and *not only/but also*. When you encounter one of these pairs, make sure the words or phrases they link are parallel. For example, instead of writing, "The place where I live is neither my choice nor is it my destiny," you would write "the place where I live is neither my choice nor my destiny."

>> **Look for two complete sentences joined together.** In a sentence with two predicates, make sure the predicates are structured the same way. For example, "Sam decided to tune her car and took a shower before going out for the evening" suffers from a lack of parallelism. Parallel wording would be, "Sam decided to tune her car and take a shower before going out for the evening."

Casing pronouns

Pronouns have *case*, which refers to using *he* versus *him*, *she* versus *her*, *they* versus *them*, *it* versus . . . well, *it* is the same. Anyway, the rule is simple: Use a subject pronoun (*he, she, they*) for the subject, and an object pronoun (*him, her, them*) for almost everything else. Here's how you tell the difference:

>> **Identify the subject and the object.** The *subject* is the one that's doing something, and the *object* is the target of the action. For example, if you see, "The referee penalized the player," the *referee* is the subject, and the *player* is the object. In pronoun case, this sentence would read, "*He* penalized *him*."

>> **Isolate the pronoun.** If you see, "The proctor gave the test to three boys and she," you may not notice the error. Cut out "the three boys," however, and you have, "The proctor gave the test to *she*." Now the error is easier to spot: The sentence should read, "The proctor gave the test to *her*."

REMEMBER

One thing: The pronoun *must* be clear. Something like, "Mary and Sandy each used the book, and she aced the exam!" won't fly.

Using punctuation

Some punctuation also appears in the SAT Reading and Writing section. Here is what you need to know:

>> **Join sentences correctly.** Sometimes a comma and a *conjunction* (joining word) — for example, *and, or, but,* and *nor* — do the job, and sometimes you need a semicolon. Note that a comma alone doesn't do the trick: You also need the conjunction. Transition words (*consequently, therefore, nevertheless, however*) look like they could join two sentences, but they can't — they need a semicolon. More on the semicolon next.

>> **Know semicolons.** The *semicolon* (;) joins two complete sentences. It takes the place of the *comma* with *and*. "The dog ran outside, *and* the cat chased it" could also be correctly stated as, "The dog ran outside; the cat chased it." Typically, the SAT has a complete sentence *before* the semicolon — you need to make sure there's a complete sentence *after* it. Also, the semicolon never goes with the word *and* — the semicolon takes the place of "and".

>> **Punctuate descriptions correctly.** If the description is essential to the meaning of the sentence — you don't know what you're talking about without the description — don't use commas. If the description is interesting but nonessential, place commas around it.

  • For example, don't place commas around this description, because you need the George part to clarify the sentence: "The play *that George wrote* makes no mention of the SAT."

- On the other hand, place commas around this description, because the opening date isn't essential to the point of the sentence: "George's play, *which opened last Friday*, broke records at the box office."

» **Check apostrophes.** You may find an apostrophe where it doesn't belong, say in a possessive pronoun or in a simple, non-possessive plural.

- A possessive pronoun (*whose, its, theirs, his, hers, our,* and so on) never has an apostrophe.

- A conjunction that joins two words (*it's, don't, isn't, aren't*) always has an apostrophe. This is how you tell *it's* from *its*: *It's* joins *it* and *is* and gets an apostrophe; *its* is the possessive of *it* and does not have an apostrophe.

Know that *it's* with an apostrophe is the contraction of *it* and *is,* as in "*It's* parked outside." Also, *its* without an apostrophe is the possessive pronoun, as in "The dog pulled on *its* leash."

» **Use colons.** The *colon* (:) does two things. It joins two complete sentences exactly like a semicolon. Sometimes the second sentence is capitalized, but it doesn't have to be. Any time a semicolon is correct, a colon works just fine. "The dog ran outside: The cat chased it." (You'll never have to choose between a semicolon and a colon if they're both correct.) The colon can also be followed by just a word or a phrase; unlike the semicolon, it doesn't need another compete sentence. This sentence is correct: "There's one topic in math that drives me crazy: probability."

The other thing the colon does is begin a list, taking the place of *such as* or *for example.* A sentence like, "There are things on the table, *such as* an SAT, a calculator, and an aspirin," can also be written as, "There are things on the table: an SAT, a calculator, and an aspirin." The list is never capitalized (unless it has proper nouns), and the colon never goes with the words *such as* or *for example* — it takes their place.

Wording in context

The SAT asks about vocabulary in context, so you may see a word that *sounds* right but is considered wrong. These word pairs and homophones are frequent fliers on the exam:

» **Affect and effect.** The SAT *affects* your life. The *effect* of all this prep is a high score. See the difference? The first is a verb and the second a noun. Once in a while, *effect* can be a verb meaning "to bring about," as in "Pressure from college *effects* change," and *affect* can be a noun that means mood, as in "The scholarship brought a nice *affect.*" But these are rare.

» **Fewer and less.** *Fewer* is for stuff you can count (candies, teeth, cavities) and *less* is for stuff you measure (sugar, taste, toothache intensity).

» **Good and well.** In general, *good* describes nouns, and *well* describes verbs. In other words, a person or thing is *good,* but you do something *well.* Your skills are *good,* and you study *well* for the exam.

» **Ensure and insure.** You *ensure* something happens or doesn't happen, like practice *ensures* success. You *insure* something when you provide *insurance,* like the agent *insured* your truck and jet ski. That should be easy to remember.

» **Farther and further.** Take something *farther* if it's literally going a distance, like my horse ran *farther* than your horse. Take it *further* for a matter of extent, like the lawyer investigated *further.* No one messes this up.

This list obviously doesn't contain all the misused words or expressions you may encounter on the SAT tests, but these are the common offenders.

Working in the research questions

Each Reading and Writing module has about five research questions, comprised of notes on a topic, usually in bullet points, followed by a question. Like all the others in this section, read the question first.

The question may ask you to:

>> Emphasize a particular point about the notes.

>> Emphasize the aim of the study.

>> Present a study and its methodology.

>> Explain the advantage of one quality over another or explain the difference between them.

>> Emphasize the relative size, weight, capacity, or some other quality of two items.

>> Introduce a new topic to an audience.

>> Make a generalization about a study.

The steps are the same as for the other Reading and Writing questions: Cover the answer choices, read the question, read the text (in this case, bullet points), and take your best shot. Then check each answer choice, one at a time, and either cross it off or leave it as a possibility. Like the other questions, you have about a minute to get this one.

REMEMBER

The correct choice may not refer to *all* the notes. Some notes may be irrelevant.

Try this one:

PLAY

While researching a topic, a student has taken the following notes:

>> The earliest town meetings in the colonies were held in the 1630s in New England, and attendance was mandatory.

>> In the absence of a government presence, colonies held the town meetings to make rules for the community.

>> Townspeople discussed local issues of concern including schools, roads, and bridges.

>> Town meetings allowed residents to voice their opinions on public issues and to vote on laws and budgets.

>> Town meetings are considered examples of "pure democracy," because each citizen represents himself.

The student wants to make a generalization about the impact of the town meetings on American democracy. Which choice best accomplishes this goal?

(A) It is likely that town meetings served a social as well as a political purpose in the colonies as they were opportunities for hard-working citizens to gather for reasons other than religious services.

(B) Having the townspeople gather at regular intervals and directly vote on the laws governing the colony was an example of direct democracy in action.

(C) Although New England town meetings are often described as opportunities for residents to voice their opinions of public issues such as schools, roads, and bridges, it is probable that not everyone attended and that only the men were allowed to vote.

(D) Town meetings held in the colonies are historically acclaimed as a notable model of pure self-government and self-determination that guided the foundations of the independent United States of America.

Answer the question yourself: What is the general impact of a town meeting on American democracy? Maybe the town meeting was the *precursor* (beginning) of the modern democracy model. Now cross off wrong answers:

Choice (A) describes the purpose of the town meetings, but doesn't show them as leading to democracy, so cross it off. (Remember, the online SAT allows you to cross off wrong answers.)

Choice (B) describes town meetings as leading to democracy, but it's too specific. Remember, the question asks for a *generalization*. Cross out this trap answer, or you could keep it for now while reviewing the other answer choices.

Choice (C) also describes town meetings' relevance to democracy, but it digresses into detail and problems with the model. Another non-generalization, but this one is off topic. Cross it out.

Choice (D) is rather general and describes how town meetings led to democracy. You can almost hear the music. Keep this one, and go with it, as it's better than Choice (B) and is the correct answer.

You got this. A little practice is all it takes, so here you go. You're welcome.

Sorting Out Critical Thinking and Data Questions

Whether you like reading lengthy novels or spending hours scrolling through social media, or both, you are bombarded with information and data in some form every day. This will help your SAT performance, because on your exam, you'll read short passages (both fiction and nonfiction), some with graphic information, and answer a question on each passage. The previous section covered questions on grammar, main ideas, and details; this section takes things further with questions on critical thinking and data analysis.

Recognizing the question formats

Critical Thinking and Data questions appear in standard formats on the SAT. These are the question types you'll encounter:

Purpose of underlined sentence asks, as the name suggests, for the purpose of a sentence underlined within a paragraph.

Overall structure of text asks about how the text was written, such as whose point of view is expressed and whether the main idea is stated or implied.

Paired reading has two paragraphs, or texts, and asks how they fit together. For example, one text could be an example of the other, a counterargument, or a response.

Using data provides data in the form of a table or a graph, along with a question on what you can infer from it.

Strengthening or weakening a claim describes an argument or a plan, which you strengthen or weaken based on new information from the answer choices.

Using quotations for support is a variation of strengthening or weakening a claim, where the answers are quotes instead of simply information.

Logically completing the text is easy to spot because it's text that's missing the ending. It's also easy to answer, because if you understand the text, then only one answer logically completes it.

These formats may overlap. For example, you may logically complete the text based on data. What's important is that by recognizing the question format, you're one step closer to taking control of the exam and knowing exactly what to do.

Applying the strategies

Remember those strategies that I keep repeating? These are the keys to your success, and they work only if you practice them, so here they are again, summarized. Be sure to apply these strategies as you practice the questions in this block.

Remember to stick with the one-minute-per-question rule. If you're stuck, guess an answer, mark the question for review (or circle it in this book), *move on*, and come back to it later. These strategies help you keep this timing:

» **Cover the answer choices.** Use your scratch paper or hand to cover the screen. Focus on understanding the question and text without distraction from the answer choices.

» **Read the question first and *then* the text.** This way you know what you're looking for when reading the text.

» **Answer the question yourself.** Your answer won't match the correct answer, but it doesn't have to — instead, it makes the *wrong* answers stand out.

» **Check each answer and cross off wrong ones.** Remember: You're *not* looking for the right answer. You're *crossing off* wrong answers.

If you answer the question yourself, then the three wrong answers stand out like lemons on an apple tree. There will be one answer that you don't cross off, so go with that. It's all you'll have time to do.

Exploring the question formats

Since the SAT uses a standard set of question formats, you can recognize and practice them. You can go into the test knowing exactly what to expect and how to get the questions right.

Purpose of the underlined sentence

In this question, a portion of the text is underlined, and your task is to determine which answer choice most accurately states the purpose of the underlined portion in the context of the whole text.

PLAY

The following is adapted from an article titled "The Deadliest Atlantic Tropical Cyclones, 1492–1996" from the National Hurricane Center and Central Pacific Hurricane Center website.

The legacies of Atlantic tropical cyclones span many cultures and thousands of years. Early evidence of these storms predates extant weather records. <u>Geologists believe that layers of sediment at the bottom of a lake in Alabama were brought there from the nearby Gulf of Mexico by storm surges associated with intense hurricanes that occurred as much as 3,000 years ago (Liu and Fearn 1993).</u> Similarly, sediment cores from the Florida west coast indicate exceptional freshwater floods during strong hurricanes more than a thousand years ago (Davis et al. 1989).

Perhaps the first human record of Atlantic tropical cyclones appears in Mayan hieroglyphics (Konrad 1985). By customarily building their major settlements away from the hurricane prone coastline, the Mayans practiced a method of disaster mitigation (Konrad 1985) that, if rigorously applied today, would reduce the potential for devastation along coastal areas (e.g., Pilkey et al. 1984; Sheets 1990).

Which choice best describes the function of the underlined sentence in the overall structure of the text?

(A) It states a hypothesis that is challenged by evidence from Liu and Fearn.

(B) It provides definitive evidence that supports a claim first found in Mayan hieroglyphics.

(C) It offers a hypothesis that geologists have proved using geological analysis.

(D) It presents a finding that may prove to support a claim in the first sentence.

First, what do *you* think the writer wants the underlined sentence to accomplish in this paragraph? The sentence starts with, "Geologists believe," telling you that geologists *aren't certain* that the sediment in the Alabama lake came from a storm 3,000 years ago.

Next, cross off the wrong answer choices.

> Choice (A) says the sentence is challenged by evidence from Liu and Fearn, but Liu and Fearn offered this evidence, so cross it off.

> Choice (B) says the sentence provides definitive evidence, but you know this isn't the case, from your own answer, so cross this one off.

> Choice (C) says the sentence offers a hypothesis that geologists have proven, which, like Choice (B), you know isn't the case. Away it goes.

> Choice (D) says the sentence presents a finding that *may* (but doesn't definitely) prove to support the claim that cyclones have been occurring for thousands of years. Leave Choice (D), and it's the only one left, so go with it.

Overall structure of the text

This question asks you to determine the organizational pattern the writer uses for the text. For example, the text may be structured as a description, a sequence, a comparison, a cause and effect, or a problem and solution.

PLAY

This passage is an excerpt from *Middlemarch*, a novel by George Eliot (1871).

Miss Brooke had that kind of beauty which seems to be thrown into relief by poor dress. Her hand and wrist were so finely formed that she could wear sleeves not less bare of style than those in which the Blessed Virgin appeared to Italian painters; and her profile as well as her stature and bearing seemed to gain the more dignity from her plain garments, which by the side of provincial fashion gave her the impressiveness of a fine quotation from the Bible, — or from one of our elder poets, — in a paragraph of to-day's newspaper. She was usually spoken of as being remarkably clever, but with the addition that her sister Celia had more common-sense.

Which choice describes the overall structure of the text?

(A) A first-person narrator introduces herself, describes her friend Dorothy, and then begins her story.

(B) A third-person narrator describes Miss Brooke's physical appearance and her dress using biblical allusions, and then compares her to her sister.

(C) An unknown narrator comments on Miss Brooke's poverty, then her religious affiliation, and finally, her competition with her sister.

(D) The omniscient narrator compares two sisters, Miss Brooke and her sister Celia, and comments on their elaborate garments.

First, what do *you* think is the overall structure? Miss Brooke is on the level of Italian paintings, biblical quotes, and poems, plus she's clever but has less common sense than her sister.

Next, cross off wrong answers.

Choice (A) is out, as the passage doesn't have a first-person narrator. Cross it off.

Choice (B) stays, as it references Miss Brooke's biblical comparisons and her sister. Still check the other answer choices. Leave this one.

Choice (C) goes, as there's no evidence of Miss Brooke's religious affiliation or her competition with her sister. Cross it off.

Choice (D) is out, as the passage isn't a comparison of Miss Brooke and her sister Celia, plus it describes Miss Brooke's garments as being "plain," not "elaborate." Cross it off.

Paired reading

Paired reading offers two short texts. Your job, per the question, is to determine how the texts fit together. One text may be an example of the other, or a counterargument, or a supporting argument. Start with the question.

PLAY

Text 1 is an excerpt from *The Secret Life of Dust* by Hannah Holmes (Wiley). Text 2 is an excerpt adapted from the online article titled "Understand Climate Change" by the U.S. Global Change Research Program.

Text 1

One very clear message in the ice is that the Earth's climate is naturally erratic. According to the dust and gases trapped in the ice, the climate is always—always—in flux. If it's not getting warmer, it's getting colder. Year to year the shifts may be masked by an El Niño, La Niña, a Mount Pinatubo, or some other temporary drama.

Text 2

Earth's climate is now changing faster than at any point in the history of modern civilization, primarily as a result of human activities. Global climate change has already resulted in a wide range of impacts across every region of the country and many sectors of the economy that are expected to grow in the coming decades. Thousands of studies conducted by researchers around the world have documented increases in temperature at Earth's surface, as well as in the atmosphere and oceans. Many other aspects of global climate are changing as well. Human activities, especially emissions of heat-trapping greenhouse gases from fossil fuel combustion, deforestation, and land-use change, are the primary driver of the climate changes observed in the industrial era.

How would the author of Text 2 respond to the underlined portion of Text 1?

(A) By agreeing that climate is in a constant state of change but asserting that human activities have pushed the natural climate fluctuations to more serious and impactful levels.

(B) By asserting that climate change represents a temporary shift in climate patterns and with ongoing efforts, will reverse the effects of human activities.

(C) By acknowledging that climate change is a naturally occurring phenomenon and is unaffected by human activities.

(D) By disputing that climate change represents a normal pattern of temperature variability and asserting that it is solely a response to irresponsible human activity.

First, answer the question. How would the writer of Text 2 respond to the underlined statement? Maybe the author of Text 2 would agree with the underlined portion of Text 1, but with the *caveat* (condition) that the climate in flux is primarily changing in one direction, as a result of human activity.

Next, cross off wrong answers.

Choice (A) is possible: It recognizes that Text 2 accepts the concept of natural climate fluctuations but asserts that human activities have worsened the natural ups and downs of climate. Leave this one.

Choice (B) is out: It adds the unsupported element of climate shift being temporary. Whether this is true is irrelevant: Stay within the text itself, which doesn't mention this point. Cross it off.

Choice (C) asserts that Text 2 says that climate change is unaffected by human activities, but this is contradicted by the evidence in Text 2: "Human activities . . . are the primary driver of the climate changes observed in the industrial era." Cross it off.

Choice (D) states that Text 2 disputes the idea that climate change is a naturally occurring process, but Text 2 does not do this. Cross it off.

Choice (A) is the remaining answer and is the correct choice.

Using data

This question, as the title implies, asks you to draw a conclusion from the data in a graph or chart, or combine the data with the information in the text. You may also be asked to determine what *can't* be inferred from the data. A key strategy, after reading the question, is to focus on the data *first*, and the text *second*.

PLAY

Can animals predict earthquakes? Since ancient times, strange or unusual behavior in fish, birds, reptiles, and animals has been reported. In modern times, too, people have noticed what they believe to be early warning signals from their pets. In 1975, for example, snakes awoke from hibernation just before a major earthquake in China. The snakes froze to death; the weather was still too cold for them to survive.

Many pet owners firmly believe that their dogs or cats have advanced knowledge of the terrifying event that is a major earthquake. Because many animals can see, hear, and smell things beyond the range of human senses, they may detect small changes in air pressure, gravity, or other phenomena associated with earthquakes. Animals that predict earthquakes may be reacting to the P wave that humans can't feel. Researchers know that earthquakes generate two types of waves, P waves and S waves. The P wave travels faster than the S wave, which is stronger and more easily felt. If animals are indeed able to warn of earthquakes, and if scientists find an effective way to monitor the animals' signals, many lives will be saved.

Estimated Number of Deaths from Earthquakes, Worldwide, 2008–2019

2008	2009	2010	2011	2012	2013	2014	2015	2016	2017	2018	2019
88,708	1,790	226,050	21,942	689	1,572	756	9,624	1,297	1,012	4,535	244

U.S. Geological Survey/United States Geological Survey/Public domain

Which of the following best supports the researchers' conclusion based on data from the table?

(A) This research is important because each year more and more people die from earthquakes.

(B) While the number of people who die from earthquakes is consistent from year to year, reducing the number of deaths is certainly a worthwhile goal.

(C) Monitoring animals' signals will be a valuable resource even though the numbers of people who die from earthquakes is steadily decreasing.

(D) These efforts could help avoid another year like 2010, when more than 200,000 people died from earthquakes.

First, answer the question yourself: What's the researchers' conclusion with the data? Remember to focus on the data *first*, in which 2010 and 2008 were the deadliest years for earthquake deaths. Focus on the text *second*, which concludes that animal signals could help reduce these deaths.

Next, cross off wrong answers:

> Choice (A) is out, because the annual number of earthquake deaths is not increasing, so cross it off.

> Choice (B) is out, because even though reducing deaths is certainly worthwhile, the number of annual deaths isn't consistent from year to year. Cross this off.

> Choice (C) is out, because the annual number of earthquake deaths is not decreasing, so cross it off also.

> Choice (D) stays, because it supports the data (and your answer) that 2010 was a terrible year. This is the last answer standing and is correct.

Strengthening or weakening a claim

The text presents a claim, which you strengthen or weaken based on one of the answer choices. For example, take the claim that Myra came out of the kitchen, and the last donut was gone, so she must have eaten it. *Weaken* this claim by adding *new information* that changes the outcome (say, other people were also in the kitchen), so you can't say whether Myra ate the donut. *Strengthen* the claim by suggesting that *nothing else* happened that is relevant (say, no one else was home that day), so Myra probably *did* eat the donut.

WARNING

Watch out for answer choices that are out of scope, which are always wrong. For example, if Myra has a sweet tooth, it doesn't change the evidence of whether she ate the donut.

PLAY

The following passage is adapted from *U.S. History For Dummies*, by Steve Wiegand (Wiley).

Hopscotching from the British Isles to the Shetland Islands to the Faroe Islands, the Vikings arrived in Iceland about A.D. 870. Around 985 a colorful character known as Erik the Red discovered Greenland and led settlers there. Like so many things in human history, the Vikings' first visits to the North American continent were [probably] by accident.

Which of the following statements, if true, most weakens the claim that the discovery and visits of North American lands were by accident?

(A) The period of Scandinavian history to which the term Viking is applied extends roughly from the middle of the 8th to the end of the 10th or the first half of the 11th century.

(B) A Yale University map that supposedly offered verification of Viking explorations has been declared a forgery.

(C) Erik the Red lived in Iceland for a period of time.

(D) A newly discovered journal describes the Vikings having ambition to expand their territory by exploration and domination of new lands.

First, answer the question yourself. Keep your answer simple: It won't match the correct answer, but it'll highlight three *incorrect* answers. What would suggest that the discovery of North American lands *wasn't* by accident? Maybe that it was *on purpose*. See? Simple.

Now, cross off any answer choice that either doesn't fit with your answer or is out of scope.

> Choice (A) offers some historical background, but that's it — nothing about the accidental or intentional discovery of new lands. Cross it off.
>
> Choice (B) is interesting but out of scope. What does a university map have to do with Viking land discovery? Cross it off.
>
> Choice (C) is also out of scope. Places where Erik the Red lived have little to do with whether North American discovery was intentional. Cross this off.
>
> Choice (D) provides new information that the Vikings intended to visit and expand to new lands, so the discovery of Greenland and other North American lands was *not* by accident. Leave this answer, and it's the correct choice.

Using quotations for support

This is a variation of the Strengthening or Weakening a Claim question from the previous section. Not only do you strengthen or weaken the text, but you also find an example to support the text. Like all other questions in this section, read the question first, then the text, then answer the question yourself, and then cross off wrong answers.

PLAY

In a research paper, a student is reporting on the problems associated with sleep deprivation. The student has found anecdotal evidence that sleep deprivation is detrimental to physical and mental health, and that it can even be a causative factor in the onset of serious diseases.

Which quotation from an expert best illustrates the student's claim?

(A) "Lack of sleep also damages the immune system and is linked to many chronic health problems, including heart disease, kidney disease, high blood pressure, diabetes, stroke, obesity, and depression."

(B) "In a recent year, nearly 30 percent of adults reported that they slept less than six hours a night and only 31 percent of high school students got at least eight hours of sleep on an average weekday night."

(C) "Drivers younger than 25 are more likely to fall asleep while behind the wheel of an automobile."

(D) "In one study, research subjects who slept after learning a new task, retained knowledge and scored higher on tests than those who did not sleep."

First, answer the question yourself: What illustrates the claim that sleep deprivation is bad for you? Maybe that it makes you sick, or die, or crazy. Perfect answer. Now, cross off wrong answers:

Choice (A) looks good — it matches your answer and provides specifics about both physical health (heart disease, kidney disease, high blood pressure, diabetes, stroke, obesity) and mental health (depression). Leave it uncrossed, but check the other answers just to be sure.

Choice (B) is on topic and true, but it doesn't match your answer. It only says that many people have this. Cross it off.

Choice (C) is also a point related to sleep deprivation, but it doesn't illustrate the claim as well as Choice (A) does. It also doesn't match your answer. Cross it off.

Choice (D) says quite the opposite of your answer. Don't fall into "the choice that is close, but wrong" trap. Instead, cross it off.

The remaining answer is Choice (A), which is the correct answer.

Completing the text logically

With these questions, the text ends with an incomplete sentence, and you select the answer that best completes the logic of the sentence and the text. Think of what the text is trying to say and think to yourself what makes the most sense (in other words, answer the question yourself), before crossing off wrong answers.

PLAY

The following is adapted from *Sherlock Holmes For Dummies* by Steven Doyle and David A. Crowder (Wiley). Note: Arthur Conan Doyle's Sherlock Holmes first appeared in 1887, in a series of short stories published in *The Strand Magazine*.

The public was wildly enthusiastic about Sherlock Holmes, but one man didn't share that feeling. Incredibly, it was Arthur Conan Doyle himself. He had greater ambitions in mind as a writer; he believed he'd make his mark in literature by writing historical novels. Once Doyle began to see the detective as an impediment to his work instead of part of it, he found a way to make sure Holmes never bothered him again: he killed him off. However, Doyle never realized how popular Sherlock Holmes was until he killed him. Over 20,000 people _____.

Which choice most logically completes the text?

(A) vowed that they would never read a Sherlock Holmes story again.

(B) had never read a Sherlock Holmes story, and now they never would.

(C) canceled their subscriptions to *The Strand Magazine* in protest.

(D) preferred to read Doyle's historical novels than his detective stories.

What's the author trying to say? That Sherlock Holmes was a remarkably popular character. So, what would 20,000 people do to make the point that they didn't want to read that Sherlock was killed? Maybe protest somehow.

Now cross off the wrong answers.

Choice (A) isn't logical. Never reading another Sherlock story isn't much of a protest if no more stories are being written. Cross it off.

Choice (B) isn't logical either. If the people had never read a Sherlock story, they wouldn't be concerned if the stories ended. Cross it out.

Choice (C) is logical. The 20,000 people protested Sherlock's death by canceling their subscriptions to the magazine in which the stories appeared. Leave this answer.

Choice (D) isn't logical. If people prefer to read Doyle's historical novels to his detective stories, then they're not really protesting anything. Cross it out.

Choice (C) remains and is the correct answer.

Practicing with Sample Questions

Throughout this block, I led you through the process of analyzing and answering a wide variety of Reading and Writing questions. The time has come to practice answering similar questions on your own.

English vocabulary and conventions questions

PLAY

The following except is from *Bacteria in Daily Life* by Mrs. Percy Frankland (1903).

1. Amongst some of the curiosities to be found on the shelves of microbe-museums may be mentioned bacteria which give out light, and thus, like glowworms, reveal themselves in the dark. These light-bacteria were originally discovered on the bodies of sea creatures, and cultures of them have been successfully photographed, the only source of light being that provided by the bacilli themselves. The amount of light _____ by a single bacillus might indeed defy detection by the most sensitive plate procurable, but when gathered in multitudes, the magnitude of which even eight figures fail to express, these phosphorescent bacteria enable the dial of a watch to be easily read in the dark.

Which choice completes the text with the most logical and precise word?

(A) evicted

(B) eliminated

(C) emitted

(D) entrusted

PLAY

2. The COVID-19 pandemic disrupted businesses across the United States. Some businesses _____ the pandemic by increasing telework, adding workplace flexibilities, or changing pay. A business's response to the pandemic often depended on a particular firm's policies, which were often extended to some or all employees in the firm regardless of individual establishment size.

Which choice completes the text with the most logical and precise word or phrase?

(A) denied

(B) adjusted to

(C) conceded to

(D) disengaged

PLAY

3. The following excerpt is from *The Decline and Fall of the Roman Empire* by Edward Gibbon (1776).

The camp of a Roman legion presented the appearance of a fortified city. As soon as the space was marked out, the advanced guard carefully levelled the ground, and removed every _____ that might interrupt its perfect regularity. Its form was an exact quadrangle; and we may calculate that a square of about seven hundred yards was sufficient for the encampment of twenty thousand Romans.

Which choice completes the text with the most logical and precise word?

(A) impediment

(B) uniformity

(C) stability

(D) obscurity

PLAY

4. The prosecuting attorney tried to get the testimony of a neighbor who claimed to have heard a woman's cry excluded from the trial. He claimed that since there was no corroboration of this information, it had no _____ on the case.

Which choice completes the text with the most logical and precise word?

(A) endurance

(B) conviction

(C) propaganda

(D) bearing

PLAY

5. The following is from a history of ancient Egypt.

Hatshepsut was the daughter of the great warrior king, Thutmosis I, and, according to some historians, was during her father's later years associated with him in the government. Along with Hatshepsut, he left two sons, and the elder of these, according to Egyptian law, _____ him. The son was, however, a mere youth, of a weak and amiable temper, while Hatshepsut, his senior by some years, was a woman of great energy, clever, enterprising, vindictive, and unscrupulous. She took the direction of affairs under her brother's reign, her influence paramount in every department of the government.

(A) succeeded

(B) evaluated

(C) criticized

(D) neglected

PLAY

6. The following excerpt is from *Travels in the Upper Egyptian Deserts* by Arthur Edward Pearse Brome Weigall.

The nights in the desert are as beautiful as the days, though in winter they are often bitterly cold. With the assistance of a warm bed and plenty of blankets, however, one may sleep in the open in comfort; and only those _____ this vast bedroom will understand how beautiful night may be.

Which choice completes the text so that it conforms to the conventions of Standard English?

(A) whom know

(B) who have known

(C) whom will know

(D) who knew

7. The International Space Station is an unprecedented achievement in global human endeavors to conceive, plan, build, operate, and utilize a research platform in space. With assembly of the station at completion, continuity of visiting vehicles, and support of a full-time crew of six, the era of utilization for research by a team of global scientists _____.

Which choice completes the text so that it conforms to the conventions of Standard English?

(A) advance

(B) advances

(C) have advanced

(D) will have advanced

PLAY

8. After celebrating our cousin's birthday with a lavish three-hour dinner, we were dismayed to find that it had started snowing. We headed home immediately because of the inclement weather _____.

Which choice completes the text so that it conforms to the conventions of Standard English?

(A) and it was late.

(B) and we were worried about the fact that it was getting later and later.

(C) but the snow had us worried about it being late.

(D) and the lateness of the hour.

PLAY

9. The following excerpt is from *The Story of Mankind* by Hendrik Willem van Loon (1921).

We know very little about the first "true" men. We have never seen their pictures. In the deepest layer of clay of an ancient soil, we have sometimes found pieces of their bones. These lay buried amidst the broken skeletons of other animals that have long since disappeared from the face of the _____ have taken these bones and have been able to reconstruct our earliest ancestors with a fair degree of accuracy.

Which choice completes the text so that it conforms to the conventions of Standard English?

(A) earth, anthropologists

(B) earth and anthropologists

(C) earth, and anthropologists

(D) earth; and, anthropologists

PLAY

10. This passage is from *Into the House of the Ancestors* by Karl Maier (Wiley).

Unlike those in some other major research centers in Africa, the scientists in Bamako are Africans, mostly Malians, but with a sprinkling of researchers from neighboring African countries. This is not a case of Europeans and Americans taking a mobile First World lab and setting it up in the African bush. _____ it is a center of scientific excellence, which is administered by Malians, and where the most immediate benefits fall to Malians, though the ramifications are invaluable to Africa and the entire world.

Which choice completes the text with the most logical transition?

(A) Rather,

(B) Therefore,

(C) Furthermore,

(D) Accordingly,

PLAY

11. Breathing technique plays the most important part in the art of swimming; _____ no one ever becomes a good swimmer unless attention is paid to the matter of breathing, which must be done with regularity and precision.

Which choice completes the text with the most logical transition?

(A) but,

(B) nonetheless,

(C) conversely,

(D) in fact,

PLAY

12. The following is from the NASA's online article titled, "Meteors & Meteorites."

While researching a topic, a student has taken the following notes:

>> Meteoroids are objects in space that range from dust grains to small asteroids.

>> Most meteoroids are pieces that have broken off from comets, asteroids, or even other planets.

>> Meteoroids are essentially "space rocks" that may contain metals.

>> Early in its history, Earth experienced many large meteor impacts that caused extensive destruction.

>> Meteors are meteoroids that enter Earth's atmosphere (or that of another planet) and burn up.

>> Meteorites are meteoroids that survive a trip through the atmosphere and hit the ground. Typically, these meteorites, which are between the size of a pebble and a fist, were formed billions of years ago.

The student wants to emphasize the difference between meteoroids and meteorites. Which choice most effectively uses relevant information from the notes to accomplish this goal?

(A) Meteors were once meteorites but when they enter the atmosphere of any planet, including that of Earth, they burn up.

(B) The composition of a meteoroids can give scientists a clue as to its age and origin, while this is not true for meteorites.

(C) Meteorites are technically larger than meteoroids because they have to be large enough to survive the damaging effects of entering and surviving a trip through the atmosphere of an asteroid or a planet.

(D) Although meteoroid is the term for any rocky object in space that has become detached from a larger object such as a planet or an asteroid, once these objects enter the atmosphere of a planet and survive the trip, they are called meteorites.

Answers to English vocabulary and conventions questions

1. **C.** The topic of the text is bioluminescent bacteria, or light-producing bacteria. The logic of the sentence indicates that the word that completes the text should mean "given off." Think of a word that you know that means "giving off light," and then look at the choices: The best word to complete the text is *emitted* (released or given off). It is not *evicted* (removed from a lodging) or *eliminated* (abolished or excluded) or *entrusted* (handed over to another).

2. **B.** The topic of the text is the effect of COVID-19 on businesses. The logic of the sentence indicates that the word that completes the text should mean "modified" or "made changes to." You can probably come up with a few words to fit that meaning. The best phrase to complete the text is *adjusted to* (changed to or adapted to). The best word or phrase is not *denied* (rejected) or *conceded to* (admitted to or allowed) or *disengaged* (disconnected).

3. **A.** The topic of the text is Roman encampments. The logic of the sentence indicates that the word that completes the text should mean an obstacle or hindrance. Think of words that you know that mean obstacle, and then look at the choices. The best word to complete the text is *impediment* (an obstacle or hurdle). The best word is not *uniformity* (sameness) or *stability* (steadiness) or *obscurity* (insignificance or murkiness).

4. **D.** The topic of the text is the connection between the testimony and the case. The logic of the sentence indicates that the word that completes the text should mean relevance or connection. The best phrase to complete the text is *bearing*. To have a *bearing* on something means to have an effect on it. The best word is not *endurance* (strength or durability) or *conviction* (strongly held belief or verdict) or *propaganda* (slanted information).

5. **A.** The topic of the text is Egyptian history. The logic of the sentence indicates that the reign of the king Thutmosis I was followed by the reign of his son. Thus, his son *succeeded* or followed or replaced his father. The other choices, *evaluated* (appraised or estimated the value), *criticized* (found faults), or *neglected* (abandoned, ignored) do not fit the context of the sentence.

6. **B.** Choice (B) completes the text so that it conforms to the conventions of Standard English. The nominative pronoun *who* is needed because it is the subject of the verb *have known*; *whom* is incorrect because it is an objective pronoun. The tense that is needed in this sentence to convey action that began in the past and continues into the present is the present perfect *have known*. Choice (D) uses the correct pronoun *who* but the incorrect past tense verb *knew*.

7. **B.** Choice (B) completes the text so that it conforms to the conventions of Standard English. The singular form of the verb *advances* is needed to agree with the singular subject *utilization*. Choice (A) incorrectly uses the plural form of the verb *advance*. Choices (C) and (D) incorrectly use the plural form of the verb *have*.

8. **D.** Choice (D) completes the text so that it conforms to the conventions of Standard English, specifically, the conventions of parallel structure. Because the *lateness of the hour* is parallel to *the inclement weather*, it is the best choice. Choices (A), (B), and (C) incorrectly use an independent clause after the conjunction, so they are not parallel to the prepositional phrase *of the inclement weather*.

9. **C.** Choice (C) conforms to the conventions of Standard English because it is punctuated correctly. Two independent clauses cannot be joined with a comma — remember the dreaded comma splice? Cross out Choice (A). The same for Choice (B), which has no punctuation between the independent clauses, and Choice (D), which incorrectly uses the semicolon and the word "and."

10. **A.** Choice (A) completes the text with the most logical transition. A transitional word of contrast is needed to complete the logic of "This is not a case . . ." "Rather, it is . . ." The other choices do not convey this logical contrast. Choice (B) *therefore* indicates *as a result*. Choice (C) *furthermore* indicates *more information*. Choice (D) *accordingly* indicates *appropriately* or *for that reason*.

11. **D.** Choice (D) completes the text with the most logical transition. The second half of the sentence reinforces the first half; thus, the transitional phrase *in fact* is the most logical choice. Choices (A), (B), and (C) all indicate a contrast between the two halves, a relationship that does not fit the logic of the sentence.

12. **D.** The question prompt indicates that the student wants to emphasize the difference between meteoroids and meteorites. Your goal is to find the relevant information from the notes that will emphasize the difference. Don't fall into the trap of thinking you must use all the information; Definitely not true! Just find the relevant notes. Choice (D) most effectively uses the relevant information to highlight the essential differences between meteoroids and meteorites — basically that meteorites are meteoroids that have survived the passage through a planet's atmosphere.

Critical thinking and data questions

Practice is always good, but the data questions in particular take more time at first but go faster with practice. Following are three data questions for you to sharpen those skills before visiting the complete sets of Reading and Writing questions in Part 4.

REMEMBER

Read the question, then focus on the data *first* and the text *second*. You can usually find the answer primarily in the data.

PLAY

1. The following excerpt is from *Novel Plant Bioresources* by Ameenah Gurib-Fakim (Wiley).

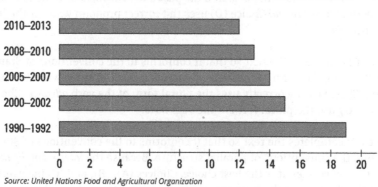

Percentage of Undernourished Persons in the World, 1990–2013

Source: United Nations Food and Agricultural Organization

The world still faces tremendous challenges in securing adequate food that is healthy, safe, and nutritious in an environmentally sustainable manner. With the growing demand of an expected 9 billion people by 2050, it remains unclear how our current global food system will cope. Currently (2014), 868 million people suffer from hunger, while micronutrient deficiencies, known as hidden hunger, undermine the development, health, and productivity of over 2 billion people.

Which of the following most effectively uses data from the graph to support the assertions in the text?

(A) The number of people who lack important nutrients is greater in rural areas than in urban areas.

(B) The percentage of the population with an adequate amount of food rose from 1990 to 2013.

(C) The number of animal species providing food for human beings is decreasing.

(D) Over 9 billion people currently face micronutrient deficiencies.

PLAY

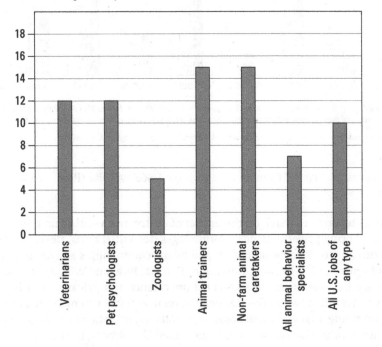

Percentage of Projected Job Growth: Animal Care and Service Workers

2. Animal care specialists, animal behaviorists, and service workers who attend to or train animals work in a fascinating field, especially for those who enjoy working with non-human species. Entry-level workers, who need a high school diploma or its equivalent, earn around $28,000 per year, though veterinarians make about $85,000 a year. In general, higher paid careers require better education and training. Overall employment of animal behavior and service workers in all the various specialties of animal behavior is projected to _____.

Which of the following most effectively uses the data from the graph to complete the text?

(A) grow by 11 percent.

(B) decrease by 15 percent.

(C) grow by 7 percent.

(D) grow by 10 percent.

PLAY

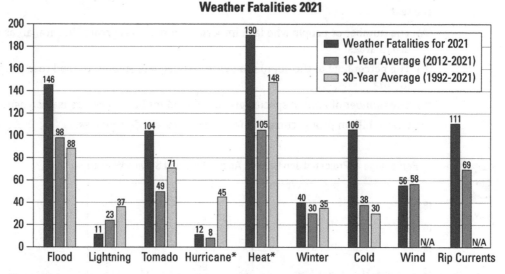

Weather Fatalities 2021

Due to an inherent delay in the reporting of official heat fatalities in some jurisdictions, this number will likely rise in subsequent updates.
The fatalities, injuries, and damage estimates found under Hurricane/Tropical Cyclone events are attributed only to the wind.

Source: National Weather Service (www.weather.gov/hazstat/)/ National Weather Service/Public domain

3. The following text is adapted from an article on the USGS website titled, "Hurricane Information."

According to a student's research on the impact of destructive weather on the U.S. population, hurricanes bring powerful winds, storm surges, torrential rains, floods, and tornadoes. A single storm can wreak havoc on coastal and inland communities and on natural areas over thousands of square miles. In 2005, Hurricanes Katrina, Rita, and Wilma demonstrated the devastation that hurricanes can inflict and the importance of hurricane hazards research and preparedness. More than half of the U.S. population lives within 50 miles of a coast, and this number is increasing. Many of these areas, especially the Atlantic and Gulf coasts, will be in the direct path of future hurricanes. Yet, while undeniably deadly, hurricanes _____.

Which choice most effectively uses data from the graph to complete the text?

(A) caused an average of 56 fatalities in the years 2012–2021.

(B) were less likely than lightning to cause fatalities in 2021.

(C) caused more deaths than tornadoes did in 2012–2021.

(D) caused fewer fatalities than heat caused over the past thirty years.

Answers to critical thinking and data questions

1. **B.** The data from the graph shows that the percentage of *undernourished* persons *decreases* from 1990 to 2012, which means that the percentage of *nourished* persons *increases* during this same time. Choice (A) is out because the graph and text say nothing about regional differences. Choice (C) goes because the graph and text don't discuss any specific sources of nutrition, and Choice (D) fails because according to the text, the population won't reach 9 billion until 2050, and when it does, there's no indication that all 100 percent will be suffering from undernourishment.

2. **C.** Choice (C) effectively uses data from the graph to complete the text. Be careful and accurate when you read the labels on the X (horizontal) and Y (vertical) axes on a graph. The sentence in the text states, "Overall employment of animal behavior and service workers in all the various specialties of animal behavior is projected to . . ." Locate the column labeled, *All animal behavior specialists*, which shows the 7 percent increase.

3. **D.** Choice (D) describes data that accurately completes the text. Choice (A) is not an accurate reading of the data; hurricanes caused an average of 8 deaths in 2012–2021. Choice (B) is also inaccurate; in 2021, lightning caused 11 deaths and hurricanes caused 12 deaths. Choice (C) is inaccurate because in 2012–2021, tornadoes caused 49 deaths and hurricanes caused 8. Only Choice (D) is accurate: Heat caused 148 deaths while hurricanes caused 45.

Block 3
Math Section

On to the math portion of the SAT. After an hour of SAT verbal, you're doing great! You've practiced and applied the strategies from this book. Now you get a well-earned 10-minute break before running for another hour or so of math. You got this.

To boost your math score, you need to revisit topics that you may not have seen since freshman year, along with the various ways that the SAT frames the question. Practice is good too — in fact, practice is the best way to get ahead. This section covers the topics you're likely to see along with plenty of targeted practice and review.

Adopting Effective Test-Taking Strategies

The SAT has two Math modules, back-to-back. On the computer version of the test, each module features 22 questions (44 questions total), all of which you can answer with the help of the built-in on-screen calculator. If you practice with the paper-based tests from the College Board, each practice Math module has 27 questions, and you're allowed to use your own calculator on the portion of the test labeled "Math Test — calculator." (For details, review the College Board's SAT Calculator Policy at https://satsuite.collegeboard.org/sat/what-to-bring-do/calculator-policy.)

Difficulty is relative. A question that's easy for you may be challenging for your friend, and vice versa. It doesn't matter anyway, because if you know what to do, the question is easy. What determines the question's difficulty in the context of the SAT? Difficulty is estimated from the number of students who miss the question during a trial, so a "difficult" question on the SAT is simply one more students missed. If you know how to approach the question, which you will after completing this block, the question is easy.

Furthermore, if you know how to approach an SAT Math question, then it takes less than a minute to answer. This means that if you know what to do, you can answer all the math questions easily and without rushing. And this leads to the first two nuggets of wisdom:

>> **Make each question easy by knowing what you're doing.** SAT Math covers only a limited number of math topics, and they're all topics that you should have seen in high school *and* are recapped in this block. Plenty of math topics, such as matrices, which appear on the ACT, are not covered on the SAT.

>> **Don't rush, because you'll make all kinds of mistakes.** Instead, to speed up your progress through the test, make sure you don't get stuck. The way you don't get stuck is by *knowing what you're doing.* Then you'll answer all the questions easily with time to spare.

Here are more bits of wisdom (also known as SAT Math Strategies) along those same lines:

>> **Don't take more than a minute on any one question.** If you don't know how to answer the question, that's okay. Here's what to do:

  ● Guess an answer.

  ● Mark the question for review.

  ● Move on to the next question.

  ● Come back to this question at the end of the module.

>> **If you find yourself working a lot of math, you missed what the question is asking.** An SAT Math question is more like a puzzle than a math problem. It never takes a lot of math work, but it may take a strategic approach based on the concept. If you understand the question and set it up correctly, everything cancels and works out nicely. On the other hand, if you're working a lot of math, step back and follow the preceding strategy: Take a guess, move on, and come back to this question at the end of the module. You'll probably spot how to work the question on this second look.

>> **Tackle the easy questions first.** A question that you answer quickly is worth the same number of points as one that takes more time, so work the questions you know first! Then go back to the time-consumers.

>> **Write clearly on your scratch paper.** Leave enough room for large, clear drawings, and make sure your text is legible. I have students mix up 5 and *s* all the time, along with the number 1 and lower-case letter *L*. Write 5 large and the *s* small, your letter *L* as a cursive loop, like ℓ, and your *t* with the hook bottom, so it doesn't look like a plus symbol (+).

>> **If you're almost out of time, click to the end and guess on 'em all.** Really, this shouldn't happen. If you practice the skills taught in the next few sections, you'll be fine — but just in case! Take the plunge and guess through the end of the test. A wrong answer is no worse than an unanswered one, so you may as well take a shot at getting it right.

Starting with formulas

The button marked Reference on the top right of the screen brings up a set of standard math formulas and equations to help you solve the problems. You'll probably forget it's there — almost everyone does — but these formulas, shown in Figure 3-1, are still good to know.

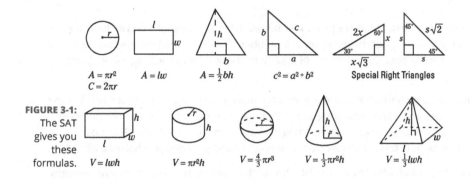

$A = \pi r^2$
$C = 2\pi r$

$A = lw$

$A = \frac{1}{2}bh$

$c^2 = a^2 + b^2$

Special Right Triangles

FIGURE 3-1: The SAT gives you these formulas.

$V = lwh$

$V = \pi r^2 h$

$V = \frac{4}{3}\pi r^3$

$V = \frac{1}{3}\pi r^2 h$

$V = \frac{1}{3}lwh$

Typing your answers

Of the 44 SAT Math questions, most are good ol' multiple choice, but some ask you to type your own answers. These questions are known as *fill-ins*. They work exactly the same as the multiple-choice questions, only you type in your answer instead of selecting it from a list.

The fill-in problems are normal math questions but with certain rules:

>> **Don't fill in a mixed number.** If you come up with $5\frac{1}{2}$ as your answer, **don't** fill in 51 / 2, because the computer will read it as "51 over 2," not "five and one-half." Instead, convert your answer to an improper fraction. Fill in 11 / 2 (11 over 2) or type in the decimal: 5.5.

>> **If more than one answer is correct, pick one.** If the answer can be either 4 or 5, go with one of those numbers and don't worry about the *other* one: The system accepts either answer as correct. That also goes for a range: If your answer is between 3 and 7, then any number between 3 and 7 is considered correct.

>> **Check whether the answer needs to be rounded.** Sometimes the answer must be an integer or a decimal rounded to a certain number of decimal places.

   For example, if you correctly calculate an answer of 1.75, and the question specifies that the answer needs to be rounded to *one* decimal place, then an answer of 1.75 is considered incorrect, while the rounded answer of 1.8 is considered correct.

>> **If your answer is a repeating decimal, type in all the digits, rounding off the last number only.** In other words, enter .3333 or .6667 (1 / 3 and 2 / 3 expressed as decimals), not .3 or .67. Note that you don't have to round the last number; if the answer is 2 / 3, you can use that, or .6666, or .6667. Any of those is correct; it's probably best to just use the fraction.

REMEMBER

Don't worry if you get more than one possible answer. Some fill-in questions have several possible right answers. (Usually those problems read something like, "what is one possible value of . . .") Just pick one answer and you're set.

Reviewing the SAT Math topics

Worried? Don't be. What's important to know is that *certain math topics are on the SAT, and certain math topics aren't.* If you know which ones are on the test, and the way that the SAT frames questions in those topic areas, then each answer is within your reach. The math topics covered on the SAT are summarized below and explored in more depth throughout this block:

>> **Numbers and operations:** These are about a quarter of the math questions. Basically, anything that doesn't involve an *x* or a drawing falls into this category, which includes whole number operations, fractions, ratios, exponents, and radicals. Of these, ratios and exponents are typically the most common.

>> **Algebra and functions:** These are just under half of the math questions and include anything with an *x* or any other letter that represents a number. The most commonly occurring algebra topics include linear equations, systems of equations (basically two linear equations), and parabolas.

>> **Geometry and trigonometry:** These are about a quarter of the math questions and include the typical circles and trapezoids along with 3-D shapes such as cubes and cylinders. Questions may involve subtracting the areas or volumes of shapes, and just a little trig. The most common questions in this group involve triangles and parts of circles (like half of a wheel).

>> **Statistics and probability:** These are just a few of the math questions and involve averages and graphs, including scatter plots. The most common questions in this group are definitely the graphs.

TIP

The SAT Math throws the occasional curveball question, typically related to an unusual topic on the edge or just outside the scope of SAT Math. These are few and far between, but if you encounter one, you know what to do: Mark it for review, take a guess, and return to it later. So, here's the wisdom of all the math summed up into one line. Are you ready? *If you know how to answer most of the math questions, you can answer them quickly and have time left over to focus on the harder questions.*

So, there you are. The secrets of SAT Math. Nice! Note that whether certain topics are more common than others varies from exam to exam, and some questions involve more than one area of math, such as geometry and algebra. These assessments and any estimated priority of each math topic are based on the review of countless SATs with students. Each exam is different, and yours may have a different mix of questions or not include all the topics — but it'll be close. Reviewing the four math topics covered in this block and answering the practice questions will prepare you well for excelling at SAT Math.

REMEMBER

CALCULATING THROUGH IT

You can use a calculator on the math. Big deal. The SAT-makers declare that you can solve every problem on the test with brainpower alone, and they're right. But there's nothing wrong with a little help. A calculator isn't the *panacea* (cure-all) for solving every math problem — your preparation is — but a calculator is a good tool to have at your disposal. Fortunately, the calculator is built right into the Math modules, so you don't have to worry about remembering to bring one.

Get used to how this new calculator works. Check out the free Bluebook practice software from www. collegeboard.org and explore the on-screen calculator. In the math section, click *Calc* to bring up the calculator with scientific and graphing capability, then click *Functions* to reveal a host of advanced capability, including trigonometry, statistics, and calculus.

Don't worry about learning any new functions, as almost all SAT Math questions can be answered without the calculator or with only basic functions. But you should know how the online calculator works, so you're not wasting time getting oriented to it during the exam.

Simplifying Numbers and Operations

Now for the first step in your SAT Math review. Not only do the topics in this section comprise about a quarter of the SAT Math questions, but they're also the foundation of the questions on other SAT Math topics. For example, you need to understand exponents and radicals, covered in this section, before you take on parabolas and trigonometry, covered in the later sections "Solving Algebra and Functions" and "Drawing Geometry and Trigonometry."

Brushing up on number types and order of operations

Before getting into the nitty-gritty of simplifying numbers and operations, refresh your memory regarding types of numbers (such as whole numbers and integers) and the *order of operations* — the rules that govern which calculations to perform first when evaluating a given mathematical expression. In this section, you receive a brief refresher course on these fundamentals.

Starting with types of numbers

The SAT Math section often refers to specific number types using terms such as "rational," "irrational," "whole," and "imaginary." Don't let this fancy math terminology throw you off your game. You need to be able to recognize different number types by name:

>> **Whole numbers:** A *whole number* is any number that doesn't include a fraction or a decimal and isn't negative, including 0.

>> **Factors:** Factors are numbers multiplied together to produce another number. For example, the factors of 16 are 1, 2, 4, 8, and 16, because $1 \times 16 = 16$, $2 \times 8 = 16$, and $4 \times 4 = 16$. Note that every number is a factor of itself: 5 is a factor of 5. To factor a negative number, include negative factors. For example, factors of –6 are 1, 2, 3, 6 and –1, –2, –3, –6.

>> **Multiples:** A *multiple* is any whole number multiplied by any other whole number. For example, multiples of 4 include 4, 8, 12, and so on. Note that every number is a multiple of itself: 7 is a multiple of 7.

>> **Prime numbers:** A *prime number* is any number that has exactly two factors: itself and 1. All prime numbers are positive, and all are odd *except* for 2, which is the only even prime number. Zero and 1 aren't prime numbers.

>> **Composite numbers:** Any whole number with more than two factors (in other words, not prime) is *composite*. If you can divide a number by a smaller whole number (other than 1) without getting a remainder, it's a composite number. Note that any composite number can be divided down to its primes. For example, 30, which is composite, can be divided down to its primes: $30 = 2 \times 3 \times 5$.

TIP

Speaking of divisibility, know these points:

- Any number whose digits add up to a multiple of 3 is also divisible by 3. For example, the digits of 789 add up to 24 ($7 + 8 + 9 = 24$); because 24 is divisible by 3, so is 789.

- Same goes for multiples of 9. If the digits of a number add up to a multiple of 9, you can divide the number itself by 9. For example, the digits of 729 add up to 18 ($7 + 2 + 9 = 18$); because 18 is divisible by 9, so is 729.

- Any number ending in 0 or 5 is divisible by 5.

- Any number ending in 0 is divisible by 10.

Consider the number 365. It's not even, so it can't be divided by 2. Its digits add up to 14, which isn't divisible by 3 or 9, so it's not divisible by those either. However, it ends in 5, so it's divisible by 5. Because it doesn't end in 0, it's not divisible by 10.

» **Integers:** Any whole number or negative whole number is an *integer*. You see integers on the number line, as in Figure 3-2. You also see non-integers on the number line, but not as often.

The farther to the right on the number line a number is, the greater it is. For example, –3 is greater than –5, because –3 is to the right of –5 on the number line.

» **Consecutive numbers:** *Consecutive* means "one after another," so *consecutive numbers* are numbers that are, well, one after another. Typically, they're just integers lined up, as in 12, 13, 14, but they can be defined and categorized. For example, consecutive *odd* numbers include 9, 11, 13, while consecutive *even* numbers of course include 6, 8, 10. If a question asks about 5 consecutive numbers starting with 7, you would write 7, 8, 9, 10, 11.

» **Rational numbers:** Any integer, along with any number that can be written as a fraction — proper or improper — or as a terminating or repeating decimal, is a *rational number*. Examples of rational numbers include $\frac{2}{3}$, a *proper fraction*; $\frac{3}{2}$, an *improper fraction*; 1.2, a *terminating decimal*; and $1.\overline{09}$ (the decimal for $\frac{12}{11}$), which is a *repeating decimal* (1.090909 . . .).

» **Irrational numbers:** An irrational number has decimals that never repeat or end. Practically speaking, you need to worry about only two kinds of irrational numbers:

- Radicals (such as $\sqrt{2}$ and $\sqrt{3}$)

- π, the ratio of a circle's diameter to its circumference (yes, it's true of *any* circle)

FIGURE 3-2:
The number line.

$$-6 \quad -5 \quad -4 \quad -3 \quad -2 \quad -1 \quad 0 \quad 1 \quad 2 \quad 3 \quad 4 \quad 5 \quad 6$$

John Wiley & Sons, Inc.

You'll typically see an irrational number in its radical form or as π, hardly as an unwieldy decimal, but the SAT may expect you to know what it is or an approximation of it.

» **Real numbers:** A *real number* is any number that appears on the number line and includes each type of number described previously, including those that are rational and irrational.

» **Imaginary numbers:** An *imaginary number* is the opposite of a real number. It doesn't appear on the number line, and though applied mathematics has other imaginary numbers, only one may appear on the SAT: the square root of –1, also known as *i*. This is further explored later in this block in the section "Simplifying imaginary *i*."

» **Undefined numbers:** An *undefined number* doesn't have a meaning. The most common undefined number, and the only one that you have to consider for the SAT, is a number divided by zero. You don't actually work with this, but if the question shows $\frac{2}{3-x}$, then somewhere in there, it's guaranteed to show $x \neq 3$ just to *make sure* that you're not dealing with that undefined number.

Here's a sample SAT question based on the concept of number basics:

If x and y are both integers where x is greater than 3 and y is less than 2, then $x - y$ *could* be

(A) 3

(B) 2

(C) 1

(D) −1

If x is an integer greater than 3, it must be at least 4. If y is an integer less than 2, it must be at most 1. To find $x - y$, just place those numbers: $4 - 1 = 3$, so Choice (A) is correct. Note that making x bigger or y smaller makes $x - y$ greater than 3, so all the other choices are impossible.

Using order of operations

How many times have your folks told you to put away your phone and start your homework because you "have to get your priorities straight"? No comment on that, but here are operations priorities in math.

Consider the problem $3 + 4 \times 2$. If you add 3 and 4 first, the result is different than if you multiply 4 by 2 first. You know *PEMDAS*, remembered by "**P**lease **E**xcuse **M**y **D**ear **A**unt **S**ally," but actually meaning "**P**arentheses **E**xponents **M**ultiply **D**ivide **A**dd **S**ubtract," which describes the *order of operations*. When faced with a multipart problem, just follow this order.

1. **Work everything in parentheses.**

2. **Calculate all exponents.**

3. **Multiply and divide, from left to right.**

4. **Add and subtract, from left to right.**

The SAT doesn't give you ambiguous math problems such as $3 + 4 \times 2$, but you still should remember to work anything in parentheses first — usually. In the later section "Solving Algebra and Functions" are examples of questions that require leaving the parentheses alone. Don't worry about that exception now — you'll see it in action later — but be aware of the intended *order of operations* in a given math problem.

Simplifying numbers and operations

Now that you're refreshed on the basics, here's a dive into some actual math topics on the SAT.

Simplifying prime numbers

As defined in the previous section, a *prime number* is any number that has exactly two factors: itself and 1. It's always positive, and the only even prime number is 2 (whose factors are 1 and 2). Any other even number has more than two factors and isn't prime. For example, 4 is divisible by 1, 2, and 4. Zero isn't prime because it isn't positive, and 1 isn't prime because it has only one factor: 1.

The secret to working with prime numbers is knowing that SAT Math typically asks only about prime numbers less than 20, so just know the first bunch: 2, 3, 5, 7, 11, 13, 17, 19. Outside that group, make sure the number is *odd*, and try dividing it by other odd numbers, starting with 3. If you can't divide it evenly, then the number is prime.

If c is the smallest prime number greater than 5 and d is the largest prime number less than 15, then the value of $c + d$ is

(A) 11

(B) 13

(C) 19

(D) 20

The answer is Choice (D), 20. The smallest prime number greater than 5 is 7, and the largest prime number less than 15 is 13. Add 7 to 13 for the answer of 20.

Prime number questions aren't that common in SAT Math, but they're worth knowing and understanding.

Simplifying percents

Percent, or *per cent*, if you remember your Latin, translates to *per 100*. That's why 50 percent is 50 out of 100, or one-half.

Taking the percent of a number is simple. To turn a number into a percent, simply move the decimal point two spaces to the right and add the % symbol: 0.5 becomes 50, and then 50%. You can also turn a percent into a decimal by moving the decimal point two spaces to the left and dropping the % symbol, as in $60\% = 0.60$. (Other examples of percents to decimals include $12.5\% = 0.125$, $0.4\% = 0.004$, and so on.) You can also turn the percent into a fraction: 60 percent literally means, "60 per 100," or $60/100$, which reduces to $3/5$. Do you convert a percent to a decimal or fraction or leave it alone? The format doesn't matter, so it depends on which you're more comfortable with and on the nature of the question.

To take the percent of a percent, simply multiply the percents, or convert them back to fractions or decimals and then multiply. For example, if 50% of the chocolates are dark chocolate, and 40% of the dark chocolates have almonds, then what percent of the chocolates are dark with almonds? To multiply as percents, go with $50\% \times 40\% = 20\%$. To multiply as decimals, use $0.5 \times 0.4 = 0.2$, and as fractions, go with $\frac{50}{100} \times \frac{40}{100} \to \frac{5}{10} \times \frac{4}{10} = \frac{20}{100}$ or $\frac{1}{2} \times \frac{2}{5} = \frac{2}{10} \to \frac{20}{100}$. Any way you cut it, the answer is 20%.

For other percentage questions, fall back on the formula you mastered in grade school:

$$\frac{\text{is}}{\text{of}} = \frac{\%}{100}$$

Suppose you're asked "40% of what number is 80?" The number you're looking for is the number you're taking the percent *of*, so x will go in the *of* space in the formula:

$$\frac{80}{x} = \frac{40}{100}$$

Now cross-multiply: $40x = 8,000$. Dividing by 40 gives you $x = 200$.

You can also consider that the percent of the whole equals the part. In other words, 40% of x is 80. Set up the equation and solve for x:

$$40\%x = 80$$
$$0.4x = 80$$
$$x = \frac{80}{0.4}$$
$$x = 200$$

One subtopic of percentages is a problem that involves a percent increase or decrease. A slight variation of the percentage formula helps you out with this type of problem. Here's the formula and an example problem to help you master it:

$$\frac{\text{amount of change}}{\text{starting amount}} = \frac{x}{100}$$

PLAY

The value of your investment in the winning team of the National Softball League increased from $1,500 to $1,800 over several years. What was the percentage increase of the investment?

(A) 300

(B) 120

(C) 50

(D) 20

The correct answer is Choice (D). The key here is that the number 1,800 shouldn't be used in your formula. Before you can find the *percent* of increase, you need to find the *amount* of increase, which is $1,800 - 1,500 = 300$. To find the percentage of increase, set up this equation:

$$\frac{300}{1,500} = \frac{x}{100}$$

First reduce the fraction:

$$\frac{300}{1,500} = \frac{3}{15} = \frac{1}{5}$$

Then cross-multiply and divide by 5:

$$\frac{1}{5} = \frac{x}{100}$$
$$5x = 100$$
$$x = 20$$

Simplifying ratios

A *ratio* compares the items of a group as a reduced fraction. For example, if there are 15 trees and 10 hammocks, then the ratio of trees to hammocks is 3:2, because the fraction $\frac{15}{10}$ reduces to $\frac{3}{2}$. Here are some further points to remember about ratios:

>> A ratio is written as $\frac{\text{of}}{\text{to}}$ or of:to.

>> The ratio *of* skis *to* poles is $\frac{\text{skis}}{\text{poles}}$.

>> The ratio *of* boats *to* trailers = boats:trailers.

>> A possible total is a multiple of the *sum* of the numbers in the ratio.

You may have a ratio question like this: At an auto show, the ratio of classic cars to concept cars is 4:5. What *could* be the total number of classic and concept cars at the auto show?

To answer this question, add the numbers in the ratio: $4 + 5 = 9$. The total must be a multiple of 9, such as 9, 18, 27, 36, and so on. Or think of it another way: The total must divide evenly into the sum of the ratio. So the total can be 27, which divides evenly by 9.

Here's an example:

PLAY

To make the dough for her signature wood-fired pizzas, Julia uses 7 cups of flour for every 5 cups of water, and she only uses whole cups. If she uses at least 10 but not more than 20 cups of water, what *could* be the total number of cups of flour and water that goes into the dough?

┌─────────────────────┐
│   │
└─────────────────────┘

The answer can be 24, 36, or 48. Add the numbers in the ratio: $7 + 5 = 12$, so the total must be a multiple of 12. If Julia uses at least 10 but not more than 20 cups of water, then she uses 10, 15, or 20 cups, so multiply the multiple of 12 by 2, 3, or 4. Any of the answers 24, 36, or 48 is considered correct, so go with one of those and you're good.

Another form of the ratio question gives you the ratio and the total, and then it asks for one of the numbers. Solve it like this:

1. Put an x by each number in the ratio.

2. Set up an equation where these x numbers add up to the total.

3. Solve for x.

4. Place the number for x back into the equation.

Go through this once and it makes sense.

PLAY

A salad uses 2 Campari tomatoes for every 3 artichoke hearts, for a total of 20. How many tomatoes and artichoke hearts are in this salad?

1. 2 to 3 becomes $2x$ and $3x$

2. Set up the equation as $2x + 3x = 20$

3. Solve for x:

$$2x + 3x = 20$$
$$5x = 20$$
$$x = 4$$

4. Place 4 in for x in the equation:

$$2x + 3x = 20$$
$$2(4) + 3(4) = 20$$
$$8 + 12 = 20$$

So, there are 8 tomatoes and 12 artichoke hearts.

Ratio questions are fairly common in the SAT Math section.

Simplifying conversions

Conversions involve transforming a quantity from one unit of measurement to another. For example, if a mile is 5,280 feet, and there are 3 feet in a yard, how long is a mile in yards? Working with conversions is simply multiplying or dividing the total number by the conversion value.

In this example, because you're converting feet to yards, divide the 5,280 feet by 3 for the number of yards:

$$\frac{5{,}280 \text{ feet}}{3 \text{ feet}} = 1{,}760 \text{ yards}$$

Here's another.

PLAY

If each quarter inch on the map represents one mile, how much distance is represented by a 3-inch segment on the map?

(A) 3 miles

(B) 4 miles

(C) 9 miles

(D) 12 miles

If each quarter inch is one mile, then one inch is four miles. The 3-inch segment thus represents 12 miles, for Choice (D).

Conversion questions are fairly common in the SAT Math section, and they can be varied.

Simplifying exponents

The *exponent* is one of the most commonly asked topics on SAT Math. Here are the basics, and later on are the SAT variations.

The *base* is the big number (or letter) on the bottom. The *exponent* is the little number (or letter) in the upper-right corner.

>> In x^5, x is the base and 5 is the exponent.

>> In 3^y, 3 is the base and y is the exponent.

Any base to the zero power equals one.

>> $x^0 = 1$

>> $129^0 = 1$

>> $0^0 = 1$

A base to the first power is just the base. In other words, $4^1 = 4$.

A base to the second power is the base times itself:

>> $x^2 = x \cdot x$

>> $5^2 = 5 \times 5 = 25$

The same is true for bigger exponents. The exponent tells you how many times the numbers are multiplied together. For example, 3^4 means that you multiply 3 four times: $3^4 = 3 \times 3 \times 3 \times 3 = 81$.

A base to a negative exponent is the reciprocal of the base to a positive exponent. A *reciprocal* is the upside-down version of a fraction. For example, $\frac{4}{3}$ is the reciprocal of $\frac{3}{4}$. An integer (except 0) can also have a reciprocal: $\frac{1}{3}$ is the reciprocal of 3. When you have a negative exponent, just put base and exponent under a 1 and make the exponent positive.

» $x^{-4} = \dfrac{1}{x^4}$

» $5^{-3} = \dfrac{1}{5^3} = \dfrac{1}{125}$

The answer isn't negative. When you flip it, you get the reciprocal, and the negative goes away. Don't fall for the trap of saying that $5^{-3} = -5^3$ or -125.

Also, if a number or variable with a negative exponent, such as x^{-4}, appears in the denominator of a fraction, such as $\dfrac{2}{3x^{-4}}$, you can make the exponent positive and move it to the numerator, like this: $\dfrac{2x^4}{3}$. Note that only the part with the exponent moves, in this case x, and not the other parts of the fraction, in this case 2 and 3.

To multiply like bases, add the exponents.

» $x^3 \cdot x^2 = x^{(3+2)} = x^5$

» $5^4 \times 5^9 = 5^{(4+9)} = 5^{13}$

» $p^3 \cdot p = p^3 \cdot p^1 = p^{(3+1)} = p^4$

» $129^3 \times 129^0 = 129^{(3+0)} = 129^3$

Don't be concerned about possibly having to multiply numbers with *unlike* bases. (You can do it by making the exponents the same but that's rare on the SAT.)

» $x^2 \cdot y^3$ stays $x^2 \cdot y^3$

» $5^2 \times 7^3$ stays $5^2 \times 7^3$ (unless you actually work it out)

To divide like bases, subtract the exponents.

» $x^5 \div x^2 = x^{(5-2)} = x^3$

» $5^9 \div 5^3 = 5^{(9-3)} = 5^6$

» $x^3 \div x^7 = x^{(3-7)} = x^{-4} = \dfrac{1}{x^4}$

» $129^2 \div 129^0 = 129^{(2-0)} = 129^2$

(That last one should make sense if you think about it. Any base to the zero power is 1, and any number divided by 1 is itself.)

Did you look at $5^9 \div 5^3$ and think that it was 5^3? Falling into the trap of dividing instead of subtracting exponents is easy, especially with numbers just begging to be divided, like 9 and 3. Keep your guard up.

You should know the common powers of 2, 3, 4, and 5:

$2^2 = 4$	$3^2 = 9$	$4^2 = 16$	$5^2 = 25$
$2^3 = 8$	$3^3 = 27$	$4^3 = 64$	$5^3 = 125$
$2^4 = 16$	$3^4 = 81$		
$2^5 = 32$			
$2^6 = 64$			

Multiply exponents of exponents, like this:

» $\left(x^2\right)^3 = x^{(2 \cdot 3)} = x^6$

» $\left(5^4\right)^3 = 5^{(4 \times 3)} = 5^{12}$

You can use the common powers to give numbers like bases:

If you have $9^5 = 3^x$, meaning what exponent of 3 equals 9^5, turn the 9 into 3^2, and solve it like this:

$$9^5 = 3^x$$
$$\left(3^2\right)^5 = 3^x$$
$$3^{10} = 3^x$$

And $x = 10$. Try this one:

PLAY

In the expression $16^3 = 2^x$, the value of x is:

(A) 4

(B) 8

(C) 12

(D) 16

Give each side the same base. In this expression, 2 probably works the best:

$$16^3 = 2^x$$
$$\left(2^4\right)^3 = 2^x$$
$$2^{12} = 2^x$$
$$x = 12$$

This matches Choice (C).

Here is a variation of the theme:

You can count bases with exponents if the bases match and the exponents match. In this example, with x^3, the base is x and the exponent is 3.

» $x^3 + x^3 = 2x^3$. This works the same way as $x + x = 2x$. You're just counting them.

» $37x^3 + 10x^3 = 47x^3$. Because the bases match and the exponents match, just add the numbers (also known as numerical coefficients) to count the instances of x^3: $37 + 10 = 47$.

» $15y^2 - 10y^2 = 5y^2$. Just subtract the numbers to count the instances of y^2: $15 - 10 = 5$.

You can't count bases with different exponents or different bases. In other words, $13x^3 - 9x^2$ stays $13x^3 - 9x^2$, and $2x^2 + 3y^2$ stays $2x^2 + 3y^2$. The bases and exponents must match for you to combine them.

There's your refresher of basic exponents, but no SAT Math question asks about exponents like that. Here is what you need to know to take on an actual exponent question:

You can apply the exponent to terms multiplied together. If x and y are multiplied together, as xy, and the exponent is applied to them, as in $(xy)^3$, this is the same as $x^3 \cdot y^3$.

>> You can multiply bases that have the same exponent: $a^4 \cdot b^4 = (ab)^4$.

>> Try it with real numbers:
$$2^2 \times 3^2 = 6^2$$
$$4 \times 9 = 36$$

You can multiply a base with an exponent by expressions in parentheses: Distribute the base with the exponent by each term in the parentheses. It's easier than it sounds:

>> To simplify $x^2(x^3 + 1)$, distribute (which means "multiply") x^2 to x^3 and 1 separately, for an answer of $x^5 + x^2$.

>> To simplify $a^3(a^4 + a^5)$, first multiply a^3 by a^4 (to get a^7) and then by a^5 (to get a^8) for a final answer of $a^7 + a^8$.

You can factor a base with an exponent from a pair of like bases with different exponents. This is simply the reverse of the previous step.

>> To factor $n^5 - n^3$, divide both n's by the same n with an exponent.

>> You could divide by n (which is the same as n^1): $n(n^4 - n^2)$.

>> You could divide by n^2: $n^2(n^3 - n)$.

>> You could divide by n^3: $n^3(n^2 - 1)$.

Factor the expression according to the question. For example, say $n^5 - n^3$ were to appear in a question, like this:

The expression $\dfrac{(n^5 - n^3)}{(n^2 - 1)}$ is equivalent to:

(A) n^3

(B) n^2

(C) n

(D) 1

You can factor $n^5 - n^3$ one of the three ways shown before. Which one do you use? Well, only one of them produces a factor that cancels with $n^2 - 1$: $n^3(n^2 - 1)$.

Now factor n^3 out of $n^5 - n^3$ and revisit the question:

$$\frac{(n^5 - n^3)}{(n^2 - 1)}$$
$$\frac{n^3(n^2 - 1)}{(n^2 - 1)}$$

Cancel the $\left(n^2-1\right)$ from the top and bottom, and you're left with n^3, which matches Choice (A).

That is how you see exponents in SAT Math. With some practice, you'll spot the trick and answer each of these in under a minute.

Exponents is a common topic in the SAT Math section, so be sure to practice.

TIP

The exponent affects only what it's touching. For example, $5x^2$ is equivalent to $5 \cdot x \cdot x$. You may wonder why the 5 isn't also squared: It's because the exponent is only touching the x. If you want to square the 5 also, put the expression in parentheses with the exponent on the outside: $(5x)^2 = 5 \cdot x \cdot 5 \cdot x = 25x^2$. This is also true with the negative sign: Put -5^2 in the calculator, and it returns -25. This is because the calculator reads -5^2 as $-(5 \cdot 5) = -25$. In other words, it squares the 5 and places the negative on it: -25. To square the entire -5, place it in parentheses and square it, like $(-5)^2$. The calculator reads this as $(-5) \times (-5)$ and returns the answer you were expecting: 25.

Simplifying square and cube roots

A *square root* refers to a quantity that, when squared, yields the starting quantity. For example, $\sqrt{16} = 4$, because $4^2 = 16$. A *cube root* is similar, except the quantity is cubed to yield the starting quantity. For example, $\sqrt[3]{8} = 2$, because $2^3 = 8$.

In math-speak, a *radical* is a root as well as the symbol indicating a root, $\sqrt{\ }$. Although most numbers have square roots that are decidedly not pretty, ($\sqrt{2}$, for example, equals approximately 1.41), most of the radicals you encounter on the SAT will either simplify nicely (such as $\sqrt{25} = 5$) or can be left in the radical form (such as $\sqrt{2}$ or $3\sqrt{5}$).

A square root always yields a positive number, because a quantity times itself is never negative. The square root of any negative number is therefore not a real number and is referred to as *i* for *imaginary*. Whereas $\sqrt{25} = 5$ represents a real number, $\sqrt{-9} = \sqrt{9} \times \sqrt{-1} = 3 \times i = 3i$ and is imaginary, covered in the next section, "Simplifying imaginary *i*."

TIP

When $x^2 = 16$, x can equal either 4 or -4, because you're not taking the square root of x^2 or 16: you're finding values of x that satisfy the equation $x^2 = 16$. $\sqrt{16}$ can only be 4, and not -4, because a square root can only be a positive number. The x^2 variation is covered further in the section "Solving Algebra and Functions."

A cube root, on the other hand, may yield a positive or negative number, because a quantity times itself three times may be positive or negative. For example, $\sqrt[3]{64} = 4$ and $\sqrt[3]{-64} = -4$, because $(-4)(-4)(-4) = -64$.

Multiplying and dividing radicals is simple, as long as they're the same type of root (in other words, square or cube). Just multiply and divide the numbers as if there's no radical: $\sqrt{5} \times \sqrt{6} = \sqrt{30}$ and $\sqrt{14} \div \sqrt{7} = \sqrt{2}$. Note that you can't add or subtract radicals. For example, $\sqrt{3} + \sqrt{5}$ stays $\sqrt{3} + \sqrt{5}$. You can, however, count radicals if they're the same: $\sqrt{3} + \sqrt{3} = 2\sqrt{3}$, in the same way that $x + x = 2x$.

To take the square root of a fraction, take the square roots of the numerator and denominator as separate numbers. For example, to take the square root of $\sqrt{\frac{4}{25}}$, take the square roots of 4 and 25 separately: $\sqrt{\frac{4}{25}} = \frac{\sqrt{4}}{\sqrt{25}} = \frac{2}{5}$

If the numerator and denominator don't square-root easily, try simplifying the fraction first: $\sqrt{\frac{50}{2}} = \sqrt{25} = 5$

You can break down any radical by factoring out a perfect square and simplifying it, like these:

$$\sqrt{27}$$
$$\left(\sqrt{9}\right)\left(\sqrt{3}\right)$$
$$3\sqrt{3}$$

and

$$\sqrt{12}$$
$$\left(\sqrt{4}\right)\left(\sqrt{3}\right)$$
$$2\sqrt{3}$$

A root can also be shown as a fractional exponent. For example, $3^{\frac{1}{2}} = \sqrt{3}$ and $5^{\frac{1}{3}} = \sqrt[3]{5}$. The denominator of the fraction becomes the *index number* (the small number outside the radical), and the numerator of the fraction stays as the exponent. For example, $7^{\frac{3}{5}} = \sqrt[5]{7^3}$.

Now try some practice:

PLAY

Which is equivalent to $5\sqrt{18}$?

(A) $15\sqrt{2}$

(B) $12\sqrt{3}$

(C) $10\sqrt{5}$

(D) $8\sqrt{6}$

Simplify $5\sqrt{18}$ by factoring out the perfect square.

$$5\sqrt{18}$$
$$5\left(\sqrt{9}\right)\left(\sqrt{2}\right)$$
$$5(3)\left(\sqrt{2}\right)$$
$$15\sqrt{2}$$

And the answer is Choice (A).

Square roots are fairly common in the SAT Math section, as are cube roots to a lesser extent.

Simplifying imaginary *i*

An *imaginary* number is a number that can't exist in real math. Applied mathematics has other imaginary numbers, but only one is likely to appear on the SAT — the imaginary number *i*, which results from the square root of a negative number.

A square root always yields a positive number because a quantity times itself is never negative. The square root of any negative number is therefore not a real number; it's *imaginary*, written as *i*. Whereas $\sqrt{4} = 2$ represents a real number, $\sqrt{-9} = \sqrt{9} \times \sqrt{-1} = 3i$. The italic *i* specifically refers to the square root of −1, so you'll see *i* defined either as $i = \sqrt{-1}$ or $i^2 = -1$, which both tell you exactly the same thing.

The most common mistake while working with i is mixing up whether the result is positive or negative. Here's a summary of how i works, but *don't memorize* this table. Instead, *understand* it.

i	result
i	i
i^2	-1
i^3	$-i$
i^4	1
i^5	i

And it repeats. Because $i^4 = 1$, any power higher than 4 is simply 1 times one of the above results. What is i^{10}? Remember you multiply exponents by adding them, so it's like this:

$$i^{10} = \left(i^4\right)\left(i^4\right)\left(i^2\right)$$
$$= (1)(1)(-1)$$
$$= -1$$

Work with i the same way that you work with x. As these are true with x:

$$2x + 3x = 5x$$
$$(3)4x = 12x$$

They are also true with i:

$$3i + 5i = 8i$$
$$(2)3i = 6i$$

One other thing: The SAT Math typically presents i in the form of a quadratic, where you multiply the expressions using the FOIL method. Quadratics are covered further in "Solving Algebra and Functions," but for now, here's a refresher on that ol' FOIL:

FOIL stands for First Outer Inner Last, which basically means multiply everything in one expression by everything in the other. To multiply these expressions:

$$(x+2)(x-3)$$

≫ Start with the First terms, x times x, for x^2.

≫ Now the Outer terms, x times -3, for $-3x$.

≫ Next the Inner terms, 2 times x, for $2x$.

≫ Then the Last terms, 2 times -3, for -6.

≫ Finally, add the pieces for a final quadratic result of $x^2 - x - 6$.

On these questions, you do this with terms containing i instead of x, but it works exactly the same way, only i^2 becomes -1. Here's how the SAT offers it. You ready?

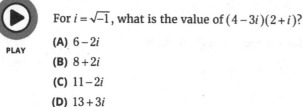

For $i = \sqrt{-1}$, what is the value of $(4 - 3i)(2 + i)$?

(A) $6 - 2i$

(B) $8 + 2i$

(C) $11 - 2i$

(D) $13 + 3i$

Don't get mad. FOIL it:

$$(4-3i)(2+i)$$
$$8+4i-6i+3$$
$$11-2i$$

Which piece by piece is:

$$(4)(2)=8$$
$$(4)(i)=4i$$
$$(-3i)(2)=-6i$$
$$(-3i)(i)=3$$

That last one, $(-3i)(i)$, is where you need to be sure the result is 3 and not −3. Work it step by step:

$$(-3i)(i)$$
$$(-3)(i)(i)$$
$$(-3)(-1)$$
$$3$$

Now that you're sure, add them up for $11-2i$, which matches Choice (C).

You're almost guaranteed to see at least one i question in the SAT Math section. More i questions are tied to conjugates, covered further in "Solving Algebra and Functions."

Simplifying projections

A *projection* is a scenario that requires you to predict a future state based on a math formula. For example, if today an orange tree is 12 feet tall, and each year it grows 3 more feet, then how tall will it be in 5 years? If t is the unit of time, in this case a year, then in t years the tree will grow $3t$ feet. If today the tree is 12 feet tall, its future height, called h, can be projected with this formula:

$$h=12+3t$$

How tall will this tree be in 5 years? Replace t with 5 and simplify it:

$$h=12+3t$$
$$=12+3(5)$$
$$=12+15$$
$$=27$$

And the orange tree will be 27 feet tall.

The SAT may ask you what the 3, the 12, or the t of the formula represent:

The 3 represents the additional number of feet per year, so that each year counted by t adds 3 feet to its height.

The 12 represents the starting height of the tree.

The t represents the time, in years, that is measured by the formula.

The SAT may also ask how the formula may change. Suppose the tree grows only 2 feet per year, instead of 3. How would you change the formula? Make the 3 into a 2, so that each year t adds only 2 feet to the tree's height:

$$h = 12 + 2t$$

That's a simple projection, and you'll see more of these with linear equations in "Solving Algebra and Functions." The SAT also gives a notoriously complex-looking projection formula, which is actually very simple after the shock factor wears off. This is the epitome of the SAT Math question that looks like madness but (1) *is workable in less than a minute* **if you know what to do,** and (2) *is simple math* **if you don't fall for the trap.**

The formula in a projection usually has an exponent that's a fraction, and that's the part that makes you jumpy. Don't be. The fraction *always* cancels out, and the rest of the formula *always* becomes simple.

Next to the orange tree is a pomegranate tree. This tree is 5 feet high, and its height is projected with this formula:

$$h = 5 + \frac{10^{\frac{t}{2}}}{t}$$

In this equation, the t exponent is divided by 2, so do you think the SAT will ask you to project the tree's height in 9 years, or 11 years? No. It'll ask you to project 2 years, or 4 years, or some number that *cancels the fraction exponent* and *keeps the math simple.*

How tall will the pomegranate tree be in 4 years? Replace t with 4:

$$h = 5 + \frac{10^{\frac{t}{2}}}{t}$$
$$= 5 + \frac{10^{\frac{(4)}{2}}}{(4)}$$
$$= 5 + \frac{10^2}{4}$$
$$= 5 + \frac{100}{4}$$
$$= 5 + 25$$
$$= 30$$

And the tree will be 30 feet tall.

TIP

Forget the calculator! You don't need it. In fact, the calculator makes this worse, because it takes you down a complex calculation path — the *trap* — that is *way off* from what you need to answer this question. Remember the wisdom from the earlier section "Adopting Effective Test-Taking Strategies": *If you find yourself working a lot of math, check your approach.*

$$f(d) = 100 + \left(2^{\frac{d}{2}} + \frac{d}{3} \right) 100$$

PLAY

This equation is a model of the projected number of seed pods given off by a certain eucalyptus tree in the spring, where d represents the number of days after the start of pollination and $f(d)$ represents the projected number of seed pods. According to the model, what is the projected number of seed pods at the end of the sixth day?

Don't be scared by the equation! Remember, the SAT gives you a number to place in that makes all the fractions cancel out. In this case, place in 6 for d, and it's almost too simple:

$$f(d) = 100 + \left(2^{\frac{d}{2}} + \frac{d}{3}\right)100$$

$$= 100 + \left(2^{\frac{(6)}{2}} + \frac{(6)}{3}\right)100$$

$$= 100 + \left(2^3 + 2\right)100$$

$$= 100 + (8 + 2)100$$

$$= 100 + (10)100$$

$$= 100 + 1{,}000$$

$$= 1{,}100$$

Projection questions are common in the SAT Math section, so practice until you're comfortable with them.

Solving Algebra and Functions

Algebra and functions are an extension of the numbers and operations covered in the previous section, and they comprise about half of the SAT Math questions. However, while numbers and operations generate only about a quarter of the SAT Math questions (as if that's not enough), it's important to understand those fundamental concepts before moving on to algebra and functions. The topics in this section truly build upon the foundation of the previous section.

REMEMBER

The SAT stays within its predefined scope of math topics and sets up the questions for easy answering if you know how to answer them. This section introduces you to the types of algebra and functions questions you're likely to encounter on the SAT and shows you how to answer each question in less than a minute.

Solving for *x*

Solving for x is just that: turning something like $2x + 3 = 5$ into $2x = 2$ and finally $x = 1$. Simple, right? But the SAT, being what it is, presents you with variations on this theme that you probably never encountered and won't see again until your Graduate Management Admissions Test (GMAT) or Graduate Record Examinations (GRE). But that's another story.

Solving for *x* with a number

To solve for x or any other variable that the question asks for, move that variable to one side of the equation, and divide both sides of the equation by the coefficient. For example, where $4x = x + 6$, subtract x from both sides of the equation for $3x = 6$. Divide both sides by 3, for $x = 2$, and the solution is 2.

A common SAT trap involves presenting you with an equation like $4x = x + 6$, but instead of asking you to solve for x, instructing you to solve for $3x$. Working this problem is just as simple, but you fall back on your tendency to solve for x instead of what the question is asking. Of course, $3x = 6$, but how many test-takers fall for the trap and respond that $x = 2$, which is true but the wrong answer?

Try this one:

$$2x + 8 = 12$$

In the above equation, what is the value of $x + 3$?

(A) 4

(B) 5

(C) 6

(D) 7

Your reflex is to solve for x, which is fine, but be sure to adjust your answer for the value of $x + 3$ and answer Choice (B):

$$2x + 8 = 12$$
$$2x = 4$$
$$x = 2$$
$$x + 3 = 5$$

Practice this so you get used to spotting the trap. You don't want to lose these easy points by sticking with a process that has been correct for most of your math life, which is solving for x by itself.

Solving for x with a y

The SAT tries to confuse you further. Just as with the projections questions in the earlier section "Simplifying Numbers and Operations," these questions appear menacing but are actually simple *if you know what to do.*

The SAT gives you an equation with two unknowns, such as $3x + 4y = 18$, asks you to solve for x, and tells you what y is: $y = 3$. Just place in 3 for y and solve for x.

$$3x + 4y = 18$$
$$3x + 4(3) = 18$$
$$3x + 12 = 18$$
$$3x = 6$$
$$x = 2$$

The first time you see one of these, you might get stuck putting it together. Of course, the letters aren't always x and y. Try this one:

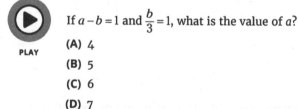

If $a - b = 1$ and $\frac{b}{3} = 1$, what is the value of a?

(A) 4

(B) 5

(C) 6

(D) 7

Start with $\frac{b}{3} = 1$ and multiply it all by 3, so that $b = 3$. There! That's the hard part. Now place 3 in for b and solve that puppy:

$$a - b = 1$$
$$a - (3) = 1$$
$$a = 4$$

And the answer is Choice (A), just like that. If this question took you longer than a minute, that's okay. That's why you're here.

Solving for *x* in a radical

Another common question type that the SAT presents, which is also just as solvable if you know what to do, is an equation containing an expression with *x* embedded within a radical. Go through it once, practice a few, and you'll have it down for the exam.

Take an equation like this:

$$\sqrt{2x^2 + 7} - 4 = 1$$

Start by keeping everything under the radical on one side of the equal sign and move everything not in the radical on the other. In this case, add 4 to both sides:

$$\sqrt{2x^2 + 7} = 5$$

Now that one side is completely under the radical, and the other is not, square both sides:

$$2x^2 + 7 = 25$$

And solve for *x* the way you usually do:

$$2x^2 + 7 = 25$$
$$2x^2 = 18$$
$$x^2 = 9$$
$$x = 3 \text{ or} - 3$$

Solving for *x* in a fraction

The SAT places *x* (or another variable) into a fraction, like this:

$$\frac{2}{15}x = \frac{2}{3}$$

First thing: When *x* is outside the fraction, move it to the top of the fraction:

$$\frac{2}{15}x \rightarrow \frac{2x}{15}$$

The basic approach is then to cross multiply:

$$\frac{2x}{15} = \frac{2}{3}$$
$$(2x)(3) = (15)(2)$$
$$6x = 30$$
$$x = 5$$

If one side of the equation is a fraction and the other side isn't, then multiply both sides by the denominator of the fraction:

$$\frac{2x}{5} = 4$$
$$(5)\frac{2x}{5} = 4(5)$$
$$2x = 20$$
$$x = 10$$

If both sides have the same denominator, you can just eliminate the denominator (which is the same as multiplying both sides by that denominator).

$$\frac{x}{7} = \frac{43}{7}$$
$$x = 43$$

Cross multiplying always works, but sometimes there's a simpler way to solve the problem. See if you can find it with this question:

PLAY

In the equation $5 - \frac{2x+2}{x+1} = \frac{9}{x+1}$, x is equal to

(A) 0

(B) 1

(C) 2

(D) 3

Note that the two fractions have common denominators, which means they can be combined easily. In this case, add the clunky $\frac{2x+2}{x+1}$ to both sides:

$$5 - \frac{2x+2}{x+1} = \frac{9}{x+1}$$
$$5 = \frac{9}{x+1} + \frac{2x+2}{x+1}$$
$$5 = \frac{9+2x+2}{x+1}$$
$$5 = \frac{11+2x}{x+1}$$

Now, multiply $x+1$ on both sides and solve for x:

$$5 = \frac{11+2x}{x+1}$$
$$(x+1)5 = 11+2x$$
$$5x+5 = 11+2x$$
$$3x = 6$$
$$x = 2$$

And Choice (C) is correct.

Sometimes cross multiplying produces a quadratic (meaning you get an x^2 along with an x), but the practice questions with quadratics are held for later in the section cleverly titled "Solving a quadratic."

Solving for *x* in a reciprocal fraction

The SAT presents you with a fraction and asks you to reciprocate it to the other side. In its simplest form, the question looks like this:

If $y = \frac{2}{3}x$, what is x in terms of y?

The most effective way to do this is to separate the fraction $\frac{2}{3}$, reciprocate it to $\frac{3}{2}$, and place it on the other side.

$$y = \frac{2}{3}x$$
$$y = \left(\frac{2}{3}\right)x$$
$$\left(\frac{3}{2}\right)y = x$$
$$\frac{3}{2}y = x$$

Technically, this is multiplying both sides by the reciprocal, but the separate-and-reciprocate approach is faster with some of the complex fractions that appear on the SAT.

Solving for more than one *x*

So far, solving for *x* has meant, for the most part, that you find *one* value for *x*. If $3x = 15$, then you know $x = 5$, and you're good. But many questions in the SAT Math section ask what *x could* be if it has more than one possible value, such as $x^2 = 9$. In this case, *x* equals either 3 or −3, and you don't know which one. Note that this is usually written as $x = 3, -3$, and it's understood that *x* has *one* of the two possible values, but not both. These multiple values are also called the *solutions* to the equation.

Solving an absolute value

Absolute value means the distance from 0 on the number line. Because distance is always positive, absolute value is also always positive. The number or value has bars on either side, like this: $|-15|$. Because −15 is 15 away from 0, the absolute value of −15 is 15, written in math as $|-15| = 15$.

A positive number works the same way. The absolute value of 3 is written $|3|$, which equals 3, because it's 3 away from 0 on the number line. The absolute value of −5 is written $|-5|$, which equals 5, because it's 5 away from 0 on the number line.

Be sure to simplify any expression inside the absolute value bars first. If you're working with $|3 - 4|$, calculate that first, for $|3 - 4| = |-1|$, and *then* take the absolute value, which in this case is 1.

If you have an *x* or other unknown inside the absolute value expression, it means that the expression is that distance from 0 on the number line, and typically could be in two separate places. For example: $|x| = 7$.

This tells you that *x* is 7 away from 0 on the number line, but you don't know whether it's on the positive side or negative side, which means that the *x* could equal 7 or −7. A couple points to glean here:

» Any *x* has *one* value: You don't know which one it is without more information. (With $|x| = 7$, something like $x > 0$ would do the trick.)

» Any absolute value is always *positive*. A distance cannot be a negative, so an equation like $|x| = -5$ is impossible, or in math, has *no solutions*.

With an expression like $|x+2| = 5$, you know that $|x+2|$ is 5 away from 0 on the number line, but you don't know which side. Therefore, you actually have two equations: $x+2 = 5$ and $x+2 = -5$. Solve them separately for the two possible values of x:

$$x+2 = 5 \quad \text{and} \quad x+2 = -5$$
$$x = 3 \qquad\qquad x = -7$$

Given $|x+2| = 5$, you know that x could equal either 3 or −7. Now try one.

PLAY

In the equation $|x-4| = 3$, x could equal:

If $|x-4|$ is 3 away from 0, solve this as two separate equations:

$$x-4 = 3 \quad \text{and} \quad x-4 = -3$$
$$x = 7 \qquad\qquad x = 1$$

Write in either 1 or 7, and you got this one right.

REMEMBER

The value of x can't be both 7 *and* 1. x has *one* value, and that's why the question reads, "x *could* equal."

WARNING

When solving an absolute value such as $|x-3| = 5$, don't write it as $x-3 = \pm 5$, which is technically true but doesn't help you. Adding 3 to both sides always leads to $x = 8$ and omits the other answer. Instead, convert the equation to $x-3 = 5, -5$, then add the 3s to get both possible values of x:

$$|x-3| = 5$$
$$x-3 = 5, -5$$
$$x = 8, -2$$

Solving a quadratic

A *quadratic* is an equation having an x^2 and often an x, such as $x^2 + 2x - 15 = 0$. Quadratics are one of the most commonly occurring SAT Math questions, and on the SAT are simpler than the ones you encounter in Algebra II. Here are some notes:

>> With a quadratic, x usually, but not always, has two possible values.

>> A quadratic results from any equation in which x is multiplied by itself. For example, cross multiplying the fractions $\frac{2}{x} = \frac{x}{2}$ results in a quadratic. (In this example, the fractions cross multiply to $x^2 = 4$, so $x = 2$ or $x = -2$).

>> When x appears more than once in a single equation or set of equations, each x has the *same* value at *one* time. If one x changes (as in a graphed equation), all the x's change with it.

>> You may need to know what a, b, and c are from a quadratic equation. These are simply the coefficients from the equation when it equals 0. In the equation $x^2 + 2x - 15 = 0$, a, b, and c are 1, 2, and −15, respectively (because x^2 times 1 is x^2, x times 2 is $2x$, and 1 times −15 is, of course, −15).

>> On the SAT, *most* quadratics are simple enough to solve without the Quadratic Formula. You *rarely* need this, but if you do, just place a, b, and c as described earlier into the formula:

$$x = \frac{-b \pm \sqrt{b^2 - 4ac}}{2a}$$

>> When you draw the graph of any quadratic equation, including $y = x^2 + 2x - 15$, in the xy-coordinate plane, the graph results in a parabola, covered in the later section "Graphing a parabola."

Approach quadratics as a two-part equation. The first involves multiplying the expressions, and the second involves factoring them. You multiply expressions using the FOIL method.

FOIL stands for First Outer Inner Last, which basically means everything in one expression is multiplied by everything in the other. To multiply these expressions:

>> $(x+2)(x-3)$

>> Start with the First terms, x times x, for x^2

>> Now the Outer terms, x times –3, for $-3x$

>> Next the Inner terms, 2 times x, for $2x$

>> Then the Last terms, 2 times –3, for –6

>> Finally add the pieces for a final quadratic result of $x^2 - x - 6$.

More common than *multiplying* expressions is *factoring* them. The numeric part of factoring is always simple: The trick is knowing the concept.

For example, given $x^2 + 2x = 15$, solve for x.

1. **Set the equation equal to 0.**

It *might* already be equal to 0, but here it's not, so subtract 15 from both sides: $x^2 + 2x - 15 = 0$

2. **Set up your answer by drawing two sets of parentheses:** $(\ )(\ ) = 0$

3. **To get x^2, the *first* terms are x and x, so fill those in:** $(x\ )(x\ ) = 0$

4. **Look at the *middle* and *last* terms of the equation:**

What two numbers add to 2 and multiply to –15? Remember that on SAT Math, *this part will be simple.* How about 5 and –3? $(x+5)(x-3) = 0$

5. **Check your work and FOIL it back out.**

Just takes a second, and it's worth knowing you did this right:

$(x+5)(x-3)$
$x^2 - 3x + 5x - 15$
$x^2 + 2x - 15$

Nice! So how does $(x+5)(x-3) = 0$ tell you what x could be? Treat it like two separate equations:

$(x+5) = 0$
$(x-3) = 0$

Meaning that x could equal either 3 or –5. In math that's written as $x = 3, -5$, and it's understood that x has only one of these two values. Also, when you graph the equation $y = x^2 + 2x - 15$, the resulting parabola crosses the x-axis at 3 and –5.

The SAT likes to explore variations of the quadratic. Here's an example:

PLAY

What are the solutions to the equation $2x^2 - 2x = 24$?

(A) 3, –4

(B) 4, –3

(C) 6, –8

(D) 8, –6

First set the equation equal to 0: $2x^2 - 2x - 24 = 0$. What next? Divide both sides by 2: $x^2 - x - 12 = 0$. *Now* you can factor it:

$$x^2 - x - 12 = 0$$
$$(x - 4)(x + 3) = 0$$
$$x = 4, -3$$

for an answer of Choice (B).

This is just one way SAT Math varies the quadratic. First you get stuck, then you work through the answer, and then you totally understand the question. Get stuck on these questions *here, now,* when it *doesn't* matter — and have them for breakfast on Exam Day. Quadratics are among the most commonly asked topics on SAT Math, so practice all the variations.

Solving the difference of squares

A *difference of squares* is a specific quadratic where a perfect square is subtracted from a perfect square, as in $a^2 - b^2$. This expression factors to $(a - b)(a + b)$, so remember it like this:

$$a^2 - b^2 = (a - b)(a + b)$$

Of course, it could be any letters, but it doesn't matter. You don't find out what a and b are, but you don't need to. Think of it like this: $(a + b)$ times $(a - b)$ equals $a^2 - b^2$. So if $(a + b)$ is 8, and $(a - b)$ is 3, what is $a^2 - b^2$? Why, it's 24.

Note that if you FOIL out $(a - b)(a + b)$, the middle terms ab and $-ab$ cancel, and the result is simply $a^2 - b^2$.

In its simplest form, the SAT asks about the difference of squares like this:

PLAY

If $c^2 - d^2 = 15$ and $c + d = 5$, what is the value of $c - d$?

(A) 2

(B) 3

(C) 4

(D) 5

Set it up and place the values that you know:

$$c^2 - d^2 = (c - d)(c + d)$$
$$(15) = (c - d)(5)$$
$$c - d = 3$$

Making the correct answer Choice (B).

Now the SAT doesn't ask about the difference of squares *quite* like that. That would be too easy! For you, it'll *still* be too easy. Anyway, the SAT embeds the difference of squares into other math topics. Try this one:

(PLAY)

If $y^2 - x^2 = 16$ and $y + x = 8$, what is the value of $\frac{2^y}{2^x}$?

(A) 2

(B) 4

(C) 8

(D) 16

Start with the $\frac{2^y}{2^x}$ as you would any other divided exponent. The same way that $\frac{2^5}{2^3} = 2^{5-3}$, $\frac{2^y}{2^x} = 2^{y-x}$. Remember doing these in the section "Simplifying Numbers and Operations"? Anyway, if $y^2 - x^2 = 16$ and $y + x = 8$, you know that $y - x = 2$, so place 2 in for $y - x$ in that exponent: $2^{y-x} \rightarrow 2^2 = 4$ for an easy, less-than-a-minute answer, Choice (B).

The difference of squares is also useful for rationalizing a fraction. *Rationalizing* means making the denominator into a rational number, which is the key to solving certain SAT fraction questions. For example, the fraction $\frac{\sqrt{5}}{\sqrt{3}}$ isn't rationalized. To rationalize it, multiply the top and bottom by $\sqrt{3}$, like this:

$$\frac{\sqrt{5}\left(\sqrt{3}\right)}{\sqrt{3}\left(\sqrt{3}\right)} = \frac{\sqrt{15}}{3}$$

The numerator isn't rational, but that's okay — the denominator is, and the fraction is rationalized.

When a polynomial expression is in the denominator, like $\frac{2-\sqrt{5}}{4-\sqrt{5}}$, rationalize it by multiplying the top and bottom by *something* that eliminates the radical on the bottom. The denominator is $4 - \sqrt{5}$, so multiply top and bottom by $4 + \sqrt{5}$, like this:

$$\frac{\left(2-\sqrt{5}\right)\left(4+\sqrt{5}\right)}{\left(4-\sqrt{5}\right)\left(4+\sqrt{5}\right)}$$

$$\frac{8+2\sqrt{5}-4\sqrt{5}-5}{16-5}$$

$$\frac{3-2\sqrt{5}}{11}$$

The top still has the irrational $\sqrt{5}$, but that doesn't matter. The bottom is fully rational, and the fraction is thus rationalized.

Solving an expression

An *expression* in math is a set of values grouped together. It's another way that the SAT packages a simple concept as a challenging question. If you cut through the façade, the actual question is simple. Sound familiar?

Say you're solving for x: $2x = 6$ becomes $x = 3$, and you know what x is because it's isolated. Do you *always* have to isolate the x? No, you can leave it in the expression, like this one: $12^x = 12^7$. You know that $x = 7$ without isolating it. Okay, here's the concept again, but on a level higher. Find the value of c:

$$x^2 - 9x + 20 = x^2 - 9x + c$$

And $c = 20$, which you know for sure even though you didn't *isolate* it. Sometimes it helps to isolate the c, by crossing off x^2 and $-9x$ from both sides, but you don't *have* to.

And there you have the basics of this topic: Two expressions equal each other, and where there's a number on one side, there's an unknown on the other, and you find the value of the unknown. Sometimes you factor one side or manipulate the equations somehow, but because this is the SAT, *you know it'll be simple even if it looks tricky.*

In this equation, where k is a constant, what is the value of k?

$$x^2 - 8x + 15 = (x-3)(x-k)$$

PLAY

(A) 5

(B) 15

(C) 25

(D) 45

Factor the polynomial on the left so it matches the one on the right:

$$x^2 - 8x + 15$$
$$(x-3)(x-5)$$

Now it looks like this: $(x-3)(x-5) = (x-3)(x-k)$.

And you know that k is 5 for an answer of Choice (A).

Another variation involves forming a quadratic and finding the values of a, b, and c. You remember a, b, and c from the discussion of quadratics all those pages ago, don't you? Copied straight from there: These are simply the coefficients from the equation when it equals 0. In the equation $x^2 + 2x - 15 = 0$, a, b, and c are 1, 2, and -15, respectively (because x^2 times 1 is x^2, x times 2 is $2x$, and 1 times -15 is -15).

You good? This is a fairly common topic on SAT Math, so be sure to practice.

Setting up equations

Setting up equations is the approach to an SAT Math question that describes a scenario, whether a story or a set of numbers, and you set up an equation to model that scenario. Sometimes you get a numeric answer, and sometimes you get an answer in terms of an unknown.

Setting up a story

A *story* is a word problem that describes a scenario, and you use this to set up an equation. For example, if Harvey handed out twice as many Twix bars this Halloween as he did last Halloween, and last year he handed out 25 bars, you know that this year he handed out 50 bars. Or, if last year Allison handed out n apples, and this year she handed out three times as many as last year, you know that this year she handed out $3n$ apples. One instance gives you a numeric answer, and the other gives you an answer in terms of an unknown.

The secret to setting up an equation is finding the verb *is*, which can be in other tenses, including *has been*, *had been*, *will have been*, and so on. When you find that verb *is* — in whatever tense — *write down an equal sign*. That gets you started.

For example: Billy *is* 3 inches taller than Henry. You can write down, $b = h + 3$. If you're not sure where to put the +3, just ask yourself, "Who's taller: Billy or Henry? (Snap fingers.) *Billy* is taller!" So add 3 to Henry.

Now try a simple one.

PLAY

The number of marbles in Box X is three times the number of marbles in Box Y. Which of the following equations is true?

(A) $3x = y$

(B) $3y = x$

(C) $xy = 3$

(D) $\dfrac{y}{x} = 3$

Translate the sentence, "The number of marbles in Box X is three times the number of marbles in Box Y" into "*x* equals 3 times *y*," or "$x = 3y$," which matches Choice (B).

Setting up equations is up there with quadratics as one of the most commonly asked topics on SAT Math. They can be varied and challenging, so you need to practice these to keep your under-a-minute average.

Setting up a sum of numbers

A *sum of numbers* is a certain type of "setting up equations" question that students tend to get stuck on, and it's commonly asked, so it's separated out here as its own topic. Basically, the SAT describes a set of numbers, gives you the total, and asks you for one of the numbers.

The question reads something like this: The sum of two numbers is 60. The first number is twice the second number. What is the smaller number?

The secret is, don't use *x* and *y*. Setting it up as $x + y = 60$ won't help you. Instead, just use *x*. If the second number is twice the first number, then that one is $2x$, and the equation becomes this:

$$x + 2x = 60$$
$$3x = 60$$
$$x = 20$$

PLAY

The sum of five numbers is 60. The first number is four times the total of the other four numbers. What is this first number?

(A) 12

(B) 24

(C) 36

(D) 48

Call the first number *x*. If *x* is four times the total of the other four numbers, then the total of those four numbers is $\dfrac{x}{4}$. Now set up the equation:

$$x + \frac{x}{4} = 60$$
$$\frac{5x}{4} = 60$$
$$5x = 240$$
$$x = 48$$

And the answer is Choice (D).

Setting up interest

Interest refers to the percent of return on a loan or investment. If you place $100 into a savings account, and in 12 months that investment is worth $105 (assuming you didn't touch it), then the additional $5 is *interest*. Start by knowing these terms.

>> **Present value (PV) or principal:** This is the starting amount of money, or the $100 in the preceding example.

>> **Future value (FV):** This is the value of the investment or loan at some future state. In SAT Math, this assumes no other transaction takes place: no fees, withdrawals, and so forth. This is the $105 in the preceding example.

>> **Interest:** This is the money earned on the investment, or $5 from the preceding example.

>> **Interest rate, or i:** This is the percent of the principal that becomes interest each term, usually a year. In the preceding example, this is 5 percent. Note that if $i = 5\%$, calculate it as $i = 0.05$.

>> **Simple versus compound:** In the second year, is the 5 percent interest rate calculated on the original $100, making it *simple* interest, or the new $105, making it *compound* interest? Finance class gets carried away with this concept, but on the SAT it stays relatively straightforward: Compound means that the interest earns its *own* interest, while simple means it doesn't.

Now to see it in action. Hopefully throughout your life, you put these concepts to work *for* you, where you save or invest money that earns interest that you *own*, rather than *against* you, where you borrow money that accumulates interest that you *pay*. Digressing slightly, but the mindset of planning ahead and preparing for success with money is right in line with planning ahead and preparing for success on the SAT. Here's how it works.

SIMPLE INTEREST

Simple interest is calculated like this:

$$FV = PV(1+i)$$

Or using the preceding example:

$$\$105 = 100(1+.05)$$

It's easier to memorize if you *understand* it. If you start with $100, how does it multiply to $105? If you multiply the $100 by the interest rate, 5 percent or 0.05, you just get the amount of interest, $5. You need to add 1 to the 0.05, so that when you multiply this by $100, you have the total *future value* of $105.

Here's a trick. The SAT expects you to know the formula for simple interest but not compound interest. If the SAT asks a compound interest question and doesn't provide the formula, just use the simple interest formula more than once. *Usually* the interest compounds only twice, so the question doesn't take long at all.

It goes something like this:

PLAY

If you place $100 into a savings account that earns 10% interest compounded annually, how much is in the account at the end of the second year, assuming the account has no other activity?

(A) $100

(B) $110

(C) $120

(D) $121

Don't worry about knowing compound interest. With only two cycles, use the simple interest formula twice. Start with the formula and place the numbers from the question to find the value of the account at the end of the *first* year:

$$FV = PV(1+i)$$
$$= (\$100)(1+0.10)$$
$$= \$100(1.1)$$
$$= \$110$$

Now do it again for the *second* year, which starts at $110:

$$FV = PV(1+i)$$
$$= (\$110)(1+0.10)$$
$$= \$110(1.1)$$
$$= \$121$$

And the answer is Choice (D).

COMPOUND INTEREST

The compound interest formula is streamlined for the SAT. Here's the thing. *Don't memorize it.* Instead, *understand it.* The SAT questions on compound interest don't expect you to come up with the formula. Instead, the answer choices will be four variations of the formula, and if you *understand* it, you can spot the three wrong variations and cross them off.

Interest that compounds once a year is calculated like this:

$$FV = PV(1+i)^t$$

It's exactly the same as the simple interest formula, only the *t* exponent stands for *time*, usually counted in years. Note that this variation exists only on the SAT. Real interest compounds more often, so that formula looks like this:

$$FV = PV\left(1+\frac{i}{n}\right)^{nt}$$

where *n* is the number of times per year that the interest compounds. For example, if the interest compounds monthly, the formula looks like this:

$$FV = PV\left(1+\frac{i}{12}\right)^{12t}$$

The *i* is divided by 12 because it's the *annual* interest divided monthly. The 12*t* is because the interest compounds 12 times per year. The *t* in this case still represents years.

Note that *n* represents the number of times that the interest compounds during the time that *i* interest accumulates. If the interest rate is *monthly*, say 0.6% per month (which is 0.006), and the interest compounds once per month, then *i* isn't divided by 12 and *t* isn't multiplied by 12: The formula would look like $FV = PV(1+i)^t$, showing a monthly cycle that accumulates *i* interest.

Here's an example. See if your *understanding* is sufficient to answer the question:

PLAY

The money in a savings account increases 0.8% each month. Which of the following equations shows the future value, FV, of the money in the account based on the present value, PV, after a period of m months?

(A) $FV = PV(0.008)^m$

(B) $FV = PV(1.008)^m$

(C) $FV = \left(\dfrac{PV}{0.008}\right)^m$

(D) $FV = \left(\dfrac{PV}{1.008^m}\right)$

It's not a math problem, remember. It's a *puzzle*. Say you start with $100, so $PV = \$100$. If i is 0.8 percent, then use 0.008 (because 0.8% = 0.008, as explained earlier in the section "Simplifying Numbers and Operations"). Which equation would lean in the direction of $FV = \$100 \times 1.008 = \$100.80$ after the first month? *Don't* do a lot of math. Instead, *estimate and eliminate*. If you have two or more answers that seem close, *then* do the math. But you won't.

> Choice (A): $FV = \$100(0.008)^m$. No matter what m is, this won't lead to $100.80, so cross it off.
>
> Choice (B): $FV = \$100(1.008)^m$. If m is 1, as it would be after the first month, then this leads to $100.80. Leave it — if you need to calculate further, you can always come back and do so.
>
> Choice (C): $FV = \left(\dfrac{\$100}{0.008}\right)^m$. Not a chance. Run it through your calculator with $m = 1$ (in other words, the first month) and you'll see why.
>
> Choice (D): $FV = \left(\dfrac{\$100}{1.008^m}\right)$. This is closer, but here's the thing. Because the denominator is slightly more than 1, each month the value of the account goes *down* slightly, not up. If a swimming pool has a slow leak, this type of equation would model the diminishing amount of water.

So what's left? Choice (B). And how much math did you do? Not much, right? You stopped after calculating the first month. *That's why this question takes about a minute.* And here's the thing, which is true for pretty much all the SAT Math. *If you understand the question, the math is simple.* It's easy to fall into the trap of doing a lot of math, so if that happens, it's okay. *Stop working on it, move on, and come back to it later.*

Interest rate questions aren't that common, but they help you understand the rate-of-change topic that follows, so they're worth practicing.

Setting up rates of change

A *rate-of-change* question is a spin on the interest rate question from the previous section, where a quantity changes slowly over time. The situation can be more complicated, and you may get two or three questions based on a single scenario. The scenarios and equations are also similar to the projections questions from the earlier section "Simplifying Numbers and Operations," only with more depth — and more questions.

A rate-of-change question describes something that grows, like the population of a city or the revenue of a business. The scenario typically provides an equation to model the rate of change, similar to the compound interest formula. Don't memorize the formula, because it changes based on the question. Instead, *understand* it.

Just look for the *starting point* and the *rate of change.* For a simple example, say that a tree is 5 feet tall and grows 3 feet each year. The SAT asks questions like these:

1. **Which equation models the tree's height after *t* years?**

   The tree's starting point is 5 and its rate of change is 3, so its height is modeled by the equation $h = 3t + 5$.

2. **What is the tree's height after 4 years?**

   $$h = 3(4) + 5$$
   Place 4 in for *t*: $= 12 + 5$
   $$= 17$$

3. **If the tree actually grows 6 feet per year, not 3, how should the equation be changed?**

   Change the $3t$ to $6t$.

A simple example indeed, but it shows the SAT questions on a rate-of-change scenario. Apply your understanding of calculating interest and the perspective of these simple questions to this example:

PLAY

Questions 1–3 are based on the following information:

Micah has a 50-pound drum of semolina in his pantry. Each week, he uses 10% of the remaining semolina in the drum for baking.

1. Which of the following equations models the amount of semolina, *s*, in pounds, remaining in the drum after *w* weeks?

   (A) $s = 50(1.1)^{w}$

   (B) $s = 50(0.1)^{w}$

   (C) $s = 50(0.9)^{w}$

   (D) $s = 50(1.9)^{w}$

2. At this rate, how many pounds of semolina will remain in the drum at the end of the second week?

   (A) 50.1

   (B) 45.3

   (C) 40.5

   (D) 35.7

3. If Micah instead obtains a 100-pound drum and each week uses 20% of the remaining semolina, then he will use exactly half of the drum

   (A) in fewer weeks than he would using 10% remaining weekly of the 50-pound drum.

   (B) in more weeks than he would using 10% remaining weekly of the 50-pound drum.

   (C) in the same number of weeks that he would using 10% remaining weekly of the 50-pound drum.

   (D) never, because at this rate he will not use half of the drum.

1. Per the scenario, Micah uses 5 pounds of semolina in the first week, because 10 percent of 50 is 5. Try out each equation to see which leaves him with 45 pounds when $w = 1$. See, the beauty of this approach is that w is an exponent, so when it equals 1, *it goes away*. You understand the question, you make it simple, you work it in *less than a minute*.

Choice (A): $s = 50(1.1)^w$. This increases the semolina to 55 pounds. Cross it off.

Choice (B): $s = 50(0.1)^w$. This leaves 5 pounds. Micah *uses* 5 pounds and should have 45 left over. Cross it off.

Choice (C): $s = 50(0.9)^w$. This leaves 45 pounds. Looks good. Don't work more math — check the next answer.

Choice (D): $s = 50(1.9)^w$. This increases the semolina to 95 pounds. Cross it off!

And the answer is Choice (C).

2. You already know how much semolina Micah has after the first week, plus you know the correct equation, so plug 45 in and run it again with w as 1. Or leave the 50 in there and set w as 2. Either way works. Here's the first way:

$$s = 45(0.9)^1$$
$$= 40.5$$

for an answer of Choice (C).

3. You could math this one out, but why? Instead, just *understand* it. If you have two drums of semolina, *regardless of the volume*, and you consume one at 10 percent per week and the other at 20 percent per week, which one will reach the halfway point first? Why, the 20 percent drum, so Choice (A) is correct.

SAT Math questions in general, but rate-of-change questions in particular, test your *understanding* of a concept more than your ability to punch numbers. This is why the calculator isn't necessarily your friend. It helps a little, as with Question 2, but if you tried answering Question 3 with the calculator, you'd *probably* get it right, but it would take a while.

Interest and rate-of-change questions borrow concepts from coordinate geometry, where you track how one number changes on its own (such as time) and causes another number to change (such as value or amount). This is a good question topic to end setting up equations and begin coordinate geometry.

Graphing coordinate geometry

Coordinate geometry refers to a drawing that results from one or more equations. You know the basic equation $y = mx + b$ that makes a line, and that squaring the x makes a parabola, and so on. If you forgot how this works, that's okay; it's all reviewed right here.

On the SAT, coordinate geometry is always two-dimensional. Geometry questions, with drawings, may have 3-D shapes, but *coordinate* geometry, on the SAT, does not. It exists on the x-y *rectangular grid*, also known as the *coordinate plane*, a two-dimensional area defined by a horizontal x-axis and a vertical y-axis that intersect at the *origin*, which has coordinates $(0,0)$, and form *Quadrants I, II, III*, and *IV*.

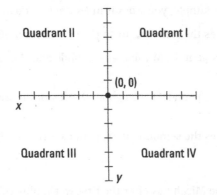

Any point on the grid has an (x,y) value, with the x indicating the horizontal position and the y indicating the vertical position. For example, this point has the coordinates $(4,5)$:

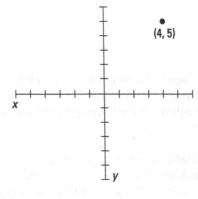

Graphing a line

A line is graphed by a *linear equation*, which is any equation with x and y and no exponents, such as $y = 2x + 1$. It can use other letters, but they're typically x and y. The equation has infinite solutions, because for any value of x, there's a matching value of y. For example, with $y = 2x + 1$, when $x = 0$, $y = 1$; when $x = 1$, $y = 3$; and so on. These x- and y-values form a line, and each x-value and matching y-value falls on the line:

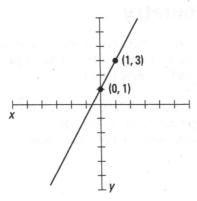

A linear equation is usually given in the *slope-intercept* form $y = mx + b$, where m is the slope and b is the y-intercept, which is the y-value when $x = 0$ and the line crosses the y-axis. With the line $y = 2x + 1$, the slope is 2 and the y-intercept is 1.

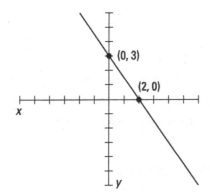

Look at the second drawing above. How do you find the equation from the line itself? Place the slope and y-intercept as the m and b, respectively, into the equation $y = mx + b$. Start with the y-intercept, which is where the line crosses the y-axis. In the drawing, the line crosses the y-axis at 3, making $b = 3$, so place that into the equation: $y = mx + 3$.

Now for the m, which is the slope. This can be found using *rise over run:* The line rises 3 and runs 2, and because it goes down, the slope is negative, so $m = -\dfrac{3}{2}$. Place that into the equation, and you have the answer: $y = -\dfrac{3}{2}x + 3$

The slope can also be found using the *slope formula*, $m = \dfrac{y_2 - y_1}{x_2 - x_1}$, which captures the *rise over run* from any two points on the line. $y_2 - y_1$ refers to one y-coordinate minus the other, and $x_2 - x_1$ refers to one x-coordinate minus the other. Place these x- and y-values into the formula:

$$m = \frac{y_2 - y_1}{x_2 - x_1}$$
$$= \frac{(0) - (3)}{(2) - (0)}$$
$$= -\frac{3}{2}$$

And you have the same result: $m = -\dfrac{3}{2}$.

Try this one:

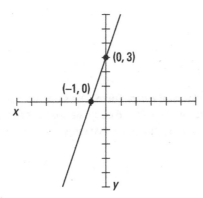

PLAY

Which of the following is the equation of the above line?

(A) $y = \frac{1}{3}x - 3$

(B) $y = -3x + 3$

(C) $y = -\frac{1}{3}x - 3$

(D) $y = 3x + 3$

Start with the bare-bones equation $y = mx + b$. The line crosses at 3, so that's the b: $y = mx + 3$. Using *rise over run*, the line rises 3 and runs 1, for $\frac{3}{1}$, or 3, and because it goes upwards from left to right, the 3 is positive. Place that for m, and you have the equation $y = 3x + 3$ for answer Choice (D).

A couple of notes before you dive into the practice questions:

» **Parallel lines have the same slope.** They may cross the *y*-axis at different points, but if they have the same slope, they're parallel.

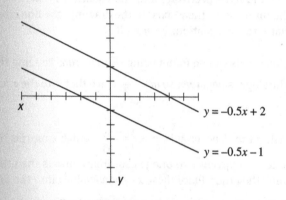

» **Perpendicular lines have the negative reciprocal slope.** Take the slope, reciprocate it, multiply it by –1, and the resulting line is perpendicular. The *y*-intercepts don't matter, even though in this drawing, they match.

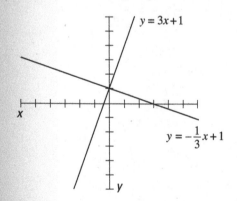

» **Linear equations don't have to use the *slope-intercept* form.** The slope-intercept form is your friend $y = mx + b$, but an equation such as $3x + 2y = 6$ counts also. To convert it to the *slope-intercept* form and find the slope and *y*-intercept, just solve for *y*:

$$3x + 2y = 6$$
$$2y = -3x + 6$$
$$y = -\frac{3}{2}x + 3$$

» **Linear equations don't need *both* x and y.** They can have just one or the other. If there's just an x, as in $x = 3$, then the line goes straight up and down, crossing the x-axis at 3 (and the slope is undefined). If there's just a y, as in $y = 5$, then the line is flat, crossing the y-axis at 5 (and the slope is 0).

» **Linear equations don't have to use *x* and *y*.** They can use any letters. Remember the tree example from the section "Setting up equations"? The tree is 5 feet tall and grows 3 feet each year: $h = 3t + 5$. If you graph this, the line would have a y-intercept of 5 and a slope of 3.

» **If it has a radical or an exponent, it's not a line.** The exponent or radical introduces a curve. In applied math it could be many things, but on the SAT it's typically a parabola or circle.

Practice working with linear equations, because you'll see plenty of these on the SAT. Also, this topic is the foundation to understanding the other topics in this "Graphing coordinate geometry" section, so it's worth practicing.

Graphing two lines

An SAT question may present two linear equations, representing two graphed lines, and ask you to find the point where the lines cross. Like everything else in SAT Math, it's remarkably simple if you know what to do. Also, this is a commonly asked question on the exam.

The SAT asks *which ordered pair satisfies* the equations or *what are the solutions* to the equations. Take the equations $y = 2x + 1$ and $y = -x + 4$. Find the solutions in three steps:

1. **Subtract one equation from the other so that you eliminate one of the unknowns.** In this example, eliminate the y:

$$y = 2x + 1$$
$$\underline{-(y = -x + 4)}$$
$$0 = 3x - 3$$

2. **Solve for the other unknown.** Here, solve for the x:

$$0 = 3x - 3$$
$$-3x = -3$$
$$x = 1$$

3. **Place that value into one of the original equations.** Knowing $x = 1$, place the 1 for x in either one of the original equations:

$$y = 2x + 1$$
$$= 2(1) + 1$$
$$= 3$$

And you have the answer: $x = 1$ and $y = 3$. This means that when you graph the two lines, they cross at the coordinates $(1, 3)$:

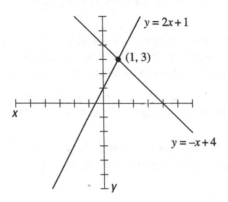

A couple of variations, which aren't common on the SAT, but you may be expected to understand:

» The equations have *infinite solutions* if they both draw the same line, because any pair of x, y coordinates that works for one equation also works for the other. If you try to solve this one, you end up with something like $0 = 0$.

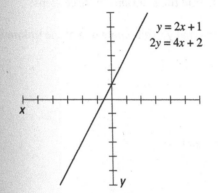

» The equations have *no solutions* if they're parallel, because there is no pair of x, y coordinates that works for *both* equations. If you try to solve this one, you end up with something like $0 = 1$.

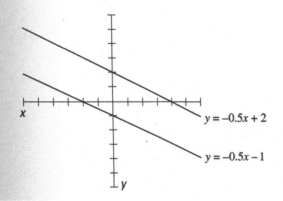

Try one:

PLAY

What is the solution to the equations $y = 2x + 3$ and $y = 3x + 7$?

(A) $(4,5)$

(B) $(4,-5)$

(C) $(-4,-5)$

(D) $(-4,5)$

Set them up and subtract them:

$$
\begin{aligned}
y &= 2x + 3 \\
-(y &= 3x + 7) \\
\hline
0 &= -x - 4 \\
x &= -4
\end{aligned}
$$

Then place -4 for x in one of the original equations:

$$
\begin{aligned}
y &= 2x + 3 \\
&= 2(-4) + 3 \\
&= -8 + 3 \\
&= -5
\end{aligned}
$$

And you have your answer: $(-4,-5)$, for Choice (C).

In a word-problem variant of this question, the SAT presents a scenario, such as two trees growing at different rates, and asks when the trees will be the same height. One tree has a height projected as $h = 3t + 5$, and the other is a smaller but faster-growing sapling, with a height projected as $h = 4t + 2$. From the equation, you know this sapling is 2 feet tall but grows 4 feet per year.

The SAT then asks you at what year the two trees will be the same height. It's exactly the same as with the (x,y) coordinates, only here, the letters are t and h, and you find the matching (t,h) coordinates. The answer is t, representing the time that's passed (and the trees' height will be h). You could use the subtraction method described earlier, but there's another way. When the h of one equation equals the h of the other, it means that the *rest* of one equation, $3t + 5$, equals the *rest* of the other, $4t + 2$. So set those equal to each other and solve for t:

$$
\begin{aligned}
3t + 5 &= 4t + 2 \\
-t &= -3 \\
t &= 3
\end{aligned}
$$

Note that a question like this always has a positive answer because it's based on a real-life scenario. A tree wouldn't be negative 3 years old.

So now you have two ways to solve this type of question, which is good, because the SAT varies this topic many ways. Encounter these variations and solve them now, when there's no pressure, so when the pressure's on, you know what to do. This topic is up there with quadratics as one of the most commonly asked question types, so learn this well.

Graphing an inequality

Graphing an inequality can be based on a linear or curved equation. Either way, the concept is the same. The SAT takes a simple equation, such as $y = 2x + 1$, and turns it into an inequality.

>> If y is *greater* than the expression, as in $y > 2x + 1$, then the inequality includes the region *above* the line, regardless of the slope.

>> If y is *less* than the expression, as in $y < 2x + 1$, then the inequality includes the region *below* the line, again regardless of the slope.

>> If it is an *or equal* inequality, as in $y \geq 2x + 1$ or $y \leq 2x + 1$, then the region *includes* the line and the line is solid; otherwise, with > or <, the region does *not* include the line and the line is dashed.

>> If it is a *horizontal* line that is *greater* than the expression, as in $y > 3$, then the inequality includes the region *above* the line; and if the horizontal line is *less than* the expression, as in $y < 2$, then the inequality includes the region *below* the line.

>> If it is a *vertical* line that is *greater* than the expression, as in $x > 5$, then the inequality includes the region *to the right* of the line; and if the vertical line is *less than* the expression, as in $x < 4$, then the inequality includes the region *to the left* of the line.

The SAT doesn't expect you to measure anything carefully. As with questions on most other topics, these questions are based on your understanding of the concepts. The SAT presents you with a scenario and asks you which inequality models it best.

For example, try one with the new sapling:

PLAY

Bill plants a two-foot-tall sapling that is expected to grow at least 4 feet per year. Which of the following inequalities best models its growth?

(A) $h > 4t + 2$

(B) $h < 4t + 2$

(C) $h \geq 4t + 2$

(D) $h \leq 4t + 2$

Cross off the wrong answers. If each year the sapling grows 4 feet or more, its height wouldn't be *less than* the expression, so eliminate Choices (B) and (D). If it grows *at least* 4 feet, then it *could* grow 4 feet, or it could grow more, so the greater-than sign is out, taking with it Choice (A). This leaves Choice (C), with the appropriate greater-than-or-equal-to sign.

Graphing an inequality isn't that common, but the scenario can be intricate. As complex as the scenario gets, remember the underlying concept is always simple. Any time you choose from equations, you *always* find the right answer by *crossing off wrong answers*.

Graphing a parabola

A *parabola* is a U-shaped curve that results from an equation in which x is squared. For example, this is the graph of $y = x^2$:

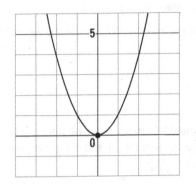

The parabola's *vertex* is the bottom center. If you were to drop a ball bearing into the U-shape, the vertex is where the ball bearing would rest. In the preceding drawing, the vertex is $(0,0)$. The official formula for a parabola is $y = a(x-h)^2 + k$, where these rules apply:

>> The vertex is at the coordinates (h,k).

>> The larger the a, the narrower the parabola. Don't worry about the a much — it's rarely asked on the SAT, but know the concept.

For example, here's the parabola graph of the equation $y = 3(x-2)^2 + 1$:

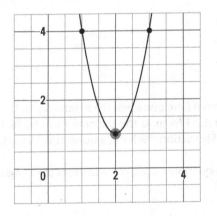

Note that it's narrower than the graph of $y = x^2$, and its vertex is $(2,1)$. Also, the h appears negative in the equation. This parabola may also appear in the form of $f(x) = 3(x-2)^2 + 1$, where $f(x)$ takes the place of y. Variations of $f(x)$ are covered in the later section "Graphing a function," but for now just treat it like this: $f(x) = y$.

The parabola equation has three forms:

» The *vertex form*, $y = (x-2)^2 - 1$, where the *xy*-coordinates of the vertex are in the equation. For example, here you know that the coordinates of the vertex are $(2, -1)$, because the *x*-coordinate appears negative, but the *y*-coordinate appears as is.

» The *standard form*, $y = x^2 - 4x + 3$, which you get from multiplying out the vertex form:

$$y = (x-2)^2 - 1$$
$$= (x^2 - 4x + 4) - 1$$
$$= x^2 - 4x + 3$$

» The *factored form*, $y = (x-3)(x-1)$, which you get from factoring the standard form. This form tells you the *x*-intercepts of the graph, which occur when $y = 0$, and in this case are 1 and 3:

$$y = x^2 - 4x + 3$$
$$= (x-3)(x-1)$$

These are three forms of the same equation, which graphs like this:

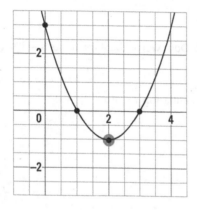

One key thing to remember is that the *factored form* gives you the *x*-intercepts. If the SAT asks for the *x*-intercepts, you can convert the standard form to the factored form by factoring it just as you would a quadratic, covered in the earlier section "Solving a quadratic." Try this one:

PLAY

At what two points does the graph of the equation $y = x^2 - 3x - 28$ cross the *x*-axis?

(A) $(3,0)$ and $(7,0)$

(B) $(4,0)$ and $(7,0)$

(C) $(-3,0)$ and $(7,0)$

(D) $(-4,0)$ and $(7,0)$

The graph crosses the *x*-axis where $y = 0$, so place 0 for *y* and factor it out. Remember when factoring this quadratic, you're looking for two numbers that add to -3 and multiply to -28.

$$0 = x^2 - 3x - 28$$
$$0 = (x+4)(x-7)$$

$y = 0$ when $x = -4$ and $x = 7$, for answer Choice (D).

The SAT may give you a quadratic equation (which graphs into a parabola) in the *standard form* and ask for the vertex. There are two ways to find this. The first is to convert the standard form to the vertex form by *completing the square*, like this:

1. **Start with the standard form.**

For example, $y = x^2 - 4x - 5$.

2. **Divide *b* (the *x*-coefficient) by 2.**

In this case, divide –4 by 2, for –2.

3. **Place *x* and the result of Step 2 into parentheses squared.**
$(x-2)^2$

4. **Take the square of the result from Step 2 and subtract it from *c* (the number without the *x*) in the original equation.**

The –2 squared becomes 4, and you subtract this from –5 in the original equation for –9.

5. **Set *y* equal to the results of Steps 3 and 4.**

You have $(x-2)^2$, so place the –9 to the right, for a result of $y = (x-2)^2 - 9$.

Here are the steps as a single set:

$$y = x^2 - 4x - 5$$
$$= (x-2)^2 - 4 - 5$$
$$= (x-2)^2 - 9$$

And you know that the vertex of this parabola is

$(2, -9)$.

The second method is to find the *axis of symmetry*, which is basically the *x*-value of a line that goes down the middle of the parabola, and using that *x* to find *y*. Both methods are useful depending on the variation of the question, but the axis of symmetry is simpler for just finding the vertex:

1. **Start with the standard form.**

In this case, $y = x^2 - 4x - 5$.

2. **Set up $\dfrac{-b}{2a}$.**

In this example, this is $\dfrac{-(-4)}{2(1)} = \dfrac{4}{2} = 2$ so the axis of symmetry is $x = 2$.

3. **Place this value of *x* into the equation.**
$$y = x^2 - 4x - 5$$
$$= (2)^2 - 4(2) - 5$$
$$= 4 - 8 - 5$$
$$= -9$$

And you know again that the vertex is $(2, -9)$. Finding the axis of symmetry is easier, but completing the square can be useful on some questions.

The parabola is very common on the SAT, but converting from standard to vertex form is not nearly as common. This process becomes easy *fast* with just a little practice, and you'll need it for certain graphing-circles questions in the next section.

TIP

When graphing an equation, the *solutions* are the values of x that cause y (or $f(x)$, covered later) to equal 0 and make the graph touch or cross the x-axis.

Graphing a circle

Many shapes can be graphed from equations, but the graphed shapes that appear on the SAT are primarily the line, the parabola, and the circle.

STANDARD FORM

This is the *standard form* of the equation of a circle:

$$(x-h)^2 + (y-k)^2 = r^2$$

In this equation, the h and the k are the x- and y-coordinates of the center, and r is the radius. Say you have a circle with a center at coordinates $(-3, 2)$ and a radius of 4. Its equation is:

$$(x+3)^2 + (y-2)^2 = 4^2 \text{ or } (x+3)^2 + (y-2)^2 = 16:$$

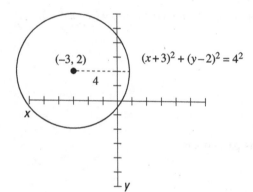

TIP

The r^2 at the end is one place the SAT tries to trip you up. If the equation of a circle is $(x+3)^2 + (y-2)^2 = 16$, the radius is **4**, not **16**.

Here's one for you to try.

PLAY

Which of the following is the equation for the graph of a circle having a center of $(-1, -7)$ and a radius of 6?

(A) $(x-1)^2 + (y-7)^2 = 6$

(B) $(x+1)^2 + (y+7)^2 = 6$

(C) $(x-1)^2 + (y-7)^2 = 36$

(D) $(x+1)^2 + (y+7)^2 = 36$

If the center of the circle is $(-1, -7)$, then inside the parentheses should be +1 and +7, so cross off Choices (A) and (C). Next, if the radius is 6, then the equation should equal 36, so cross off Choices (A) again and (B). You're left with Choice (D), which is the right answer.

GENERAL FORM

So far you've been working with the *standard form* of the equation of a circle. There's also the *general form*, which is just taking the standard form and multiplying everything out.

$$(x+3)^2 + (y-2)^2 = 5^2$$
$$\left(x^2 + 6x + 9\right) + \left(y^2 - 4y + 4\right) = (25)$$
$$x^2 + y^2 + 6x + 4y + 13 = 25$$
$$x^2 + y^2 + 6x + 4y = 12$$

The general form of the same circle is $x^2 + y^2 + 6x + 4y = 12$. Unlike the standard form, which tells you the secrets of the circle's center and radius, the general form doesn't offer much in the way of clear information about the circle.

The SAT gives you the general form of a circle, say $x^2 + y^2 - 2x + 6y = 6$, and asks for the coordinates of the center, or the radius, or something about the circle that's clear in the standard form but obscured in the general form. You need to convert the equation back to the standard form.

The way to convert the equation from the general form to the standard form is to complete the squares separately for the x part and the y part. Completing the square is introduced in the previous section, "Graphing a parabola," and continued here.

1. **Start with the general form of the circle:**

   $$x^2 + y^2 - 2x + 6y = 6$$

2. **Place the x's and y's together:**

   $$x^2 - 2x + y^2 + 6y = 6$$

3. **Place the single x and half the x-coefficient into parentheses squared and subtract the square of that number.**

   Square the –1 and subtract the result: $(x-1)^2 - 1$

4. **Do the same with the y.**

   Square the 3 and subtract the result: $(y+3)^2 - 9$

5. **Move the numbers to the right side of the equation.**

   In this case, add 1 and 9 to both sides:

   $$(x-1)^2 - 1 + (y+3)^2 - 9 = 6$$
   $$(x-1)^2 + (y+3)^2 = 16$$

6. **Convert the number on the right to its squared form:**

   The 16 becomes 4^2.

Here are the same steps as a single set:

$$x^2 + y^2 - 2x + 6y = 6$$
$$x^2 - 2x + y^2 + 6y = 6$$
$$(x-1)^2 - 1 + (y+3)^2 - 9 = 6$$
$$(x-1)^2 + (y+3)^2 = 16$$
$$= 4^2$$

You will probably see at least one graphed circle on your SAT, so prepare for it.

Graphing a function

A *function* is any kind of graphed equation that uses $f(x)$ instead of y. The equation $y = 3x - 5$ is exactly the same as $f(x) = 3x - 5$, and the value of x goes into the parentheses. So, if $x = 4$, the equation looks like this: $f(4) = 3(4) - 5$. Also, a function may use different letters, such as $g(h)$.

The SAT doesn't always give you the equation for a function. It may give you just a few values in a table, like this:

x	$f(x)$
2	3
3	8
4	5
5	11

The values may not have a pattern, so don't worry about finding one. Just know that when $x = 2$, $f(x) = 3$, and when $x = 5$, $f(x) = 11$. You won't be asked what happens when x is 3.5 or 6 or anything like that: It'll only be what's in the table.

Try this one:

PLAY

For which value of x shown in the table is $f(x) = g(x)$?

x	$f(x)$	$g(x)$
2	3	6
3	8	14
4	5	5
5	11	2

(A) 2

(B) 3

(C) 4

(D) 5

When $x = 4$, both $f(x)$ and $g(x)$ equal 5, making $f(x) = g(x)$ for answer Choice (C).

Here's another one:

PLAY

What is the value of $g(f(2))$?

x	$f(x)$	$g(x)$
2	3	6
3	8	14
4	5	5
5	11	2

(A) 2

(B) 5

(C) 6

(D) 14

From the table, when $x = 2$, $f(x) = 3$, so replace $f(2)$ with 3 in the equation. Now with the $f(2)$ out of there, you have $g(3)$, which per the table is 14. It goes like this:

$$g(f(2))$$
$$g(3)$$
$$14$$

The answer is Choice (D).

The SAT takes it one level higher. Here's how the topic works. Say you have this function:

$$f(x) = x^2 + x - 12$$

From quadratics all those pages ago, you know that the equation factors into this:

$$f(x) = (x+4)(x-3)$$

This means that $(x+4)$ and $(x-3)$ are *factors* of $f(x) = x^2 + x - 12$. It also means that when $x = 3$ or $x = -4$, $f(x) = 0$. This is also written as $f(3) = 0$ and $f(-4) = 0$.

So put all these together:

» $f(x) = x^2 + x - 12$

» $f(x) = (x+4)(x-3)$

» $f(3) = 0$ and $f(-4) = 0$

» $(x+4)$ and $(x-3)$ are *factors* of the equation.

Understand this concept back and forth, and you'll quickly and correctly answer a question that everyone around you gets stuck on and finally gets wrong. The $f(x)$ question is on the Top Ten SAT Math Topics list, so be ready.

Drawing Geometry and Trigonometry

The geometry and trigonometry on SAT Math, like the other topics on this test, go fairly in depth but have limited scope. You may encounter questions related to some topics but not others, and this boundary stays consistent with little exception.

Keep in mind that on the digital exam, you can click Reference to pop open a box of formulas and information, like this:

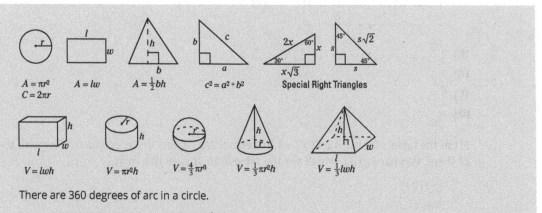

There are 360 degrees of arc in a circle.

The number of radians of arc in a circle is 2π.

There are 180 degrees in the sum of the interior angles of a triangle.

The triangle ratios are especially good to know. Of course, no one ever remembers that the formulas are there, so this section has tips and tricks to remember them.

Drawing basic shapes

Basic shapes include squares, trapezoids, triangles (which get particularly complex with side-length ratios), and circles (which get tricky but manageable with arcs and sectors). Simple strategies and some memorization are the keys here, all contained in this section.

Drawing angles

Any two lines or segments that meet or cross make an *angle*, which is the space (measured in degrees) between the lines. Understanding angles is easy when you know the different types of angles and a few key concepts.

Finding an angle is usually a matter of simple addition or subtraction. In addition to the rules in the following sections, these three rules apply to angles:

>> Angles can't be negative.

>> Angles can't be 0° or 180°.

>> Fractional angles, such as $44\frac{1}{2}$ degrees or 179.5 degrees, are rare on the SAT. Angles are typically round and whole numbers. If you're placing a number for an angle, use a whole number, such as 30, 45, or 90.

RIGHT ANGLE

Right angles equal 90 degrees and are represented by perpendicular lines with a small box where the two lines meet.

Watch out for lines that appear to be perpendicular but really aren't. An angle is a right angle *only* if the description tells you it's a right angle, you see the perpendicular symbol (⊥), or you see the box in the angle (which is the most common). Otherwise, don't assume the angle is 90 degrees.

ACUTE ANGLE

An *acute angle* is any angle greater than 0 degrees but less than 90 degrees.

Acute means sharp or perceptive, so an acute angle is sharp.

OBTUSE ANGLE

An *obtuse angle* is any angle greater than 90 degrees but less than 180 degrees.

Obtuse doesn't mean the opposite of *sharp* in a physical sense, so a dull knife wouldn't be *obtuse*, but it does mean the opposite of perceptive, so an obtuse person is . . . well, not sharp.

Angles around a point total 360 degrees, no matter how many angles there are.

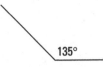

COMPLEMENTARY ANGLES

Complementary angles together form a right angle: 90 degrees.

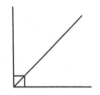

SUPPLEMENTARY ANGLES

Supplementary angles together form a straight line: 180 degrees.

Just remember that *c* stands for both *corner* (the lines form a corner) and *complementary*; *s* stands for both *straight* and *supplementary*.

TIP

VERTICAL ANGLES

Vertical angles are the opposite angles where two lines cross and have equal measures.

45° 135°
135° 45°

Vertical angles are across the *vertex* (the point where intersecting lines cross) from each other, regardless of whether they're side by side or one above the other.

TIP

TRANSVERSAL ANGLES

A *transversal* is a line that cuts through two other lines. *Transversal angles* are formed where the transversal intersects the other two lines.

A transversal cutting through two parallel lines forms two sets of four equal angles. This is also relevant to the *parallelogram* later in this section.

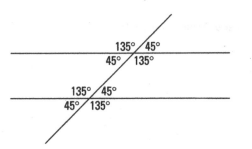

Angle concepts are mixed into other geometry and trigonometry topics, but angle-only questions come in two basic flavors. One is based on supplemental angles totaling 180°, and the other is based on angles around a point totaling 360° with the vertical angles being equal. Here they are:

PLAY

In the following image, the angles are supplementary. What is the value of x?

$(10x + 3)°$ $(7x + 7)°$

(A) 3

(B) 7

(C) 10

(D) 14

Supplementary angles total 180°, so set up an equation where the two angles total 180, drop the degree symbol, and solve for x:

$$(10x + 3) + (7x + 7) = 180$$
$$17x + 10 = 180$$
$$17x = 170$$
$$x = 10$$

And that makes Choice (C) the correct answer. Remember, an SAT Math question is always simple if it's set up correctly.

Questions on angles aren't that common in SAT Math, but angles underlie almost all the other topics related to geometry and trigonometry.

Drawing triangles

These are some standard types of triangles:

» **An *equilateral* triangle has <u>three</u> equal sides and angles.**

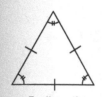

Equilateral

» **An *isosceles* triangle has <u>two</u> equal sides and angles.**

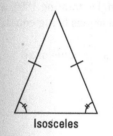

Isosceles

» A right triangle has one angle measuring 90°, which appears as a right-angle box in the drawing.

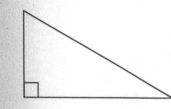

» An *isosceles right* triangle has one angle measuring 90°, and the other two angles each measure 45°.

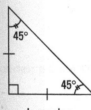

Isosceles

» **In any triangle, the largest angle is opposite the longest side.** Similarly, the smallest angle is opposite the shortest side, and the medium angle is opposite the medium-length side.

Note: In a right triangle, this largest angle is the right angle because the other two angles are each less than 90 degrees. The longest side, opposite the right angle, is the *hypotenuse*.

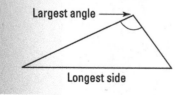

» **In any triangle, the sum of the lengths of two sides must be greater than the length of the third side.** This is written as $a + b > c$, where a, b, and c are the sides of the triangle.

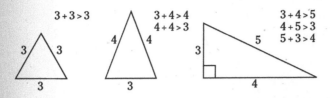

» **In any type of triangle, the sum of the interior angles is 180 degrees.**

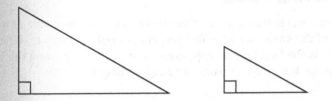

» *Similar* **triangles have the same angles but are different sizes.**

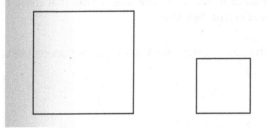

This also means that the side-length ratios are the same. Note that the term *similar* may also apply to other shapes:

CALCULATING THE AREA OF A TRIANGLE

Find the area of a triangle with $A = \frac{1}{2}bh$, where b is the *base* and h is the *height*, sometimes called the *altitude*. The *height* is the distance from any angle to the opposite base. It may be a side of the triangle, as in a right triangle:

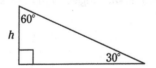

The height may also be inside the triangle, in which case it's often represented by a dashed line and a 90-degree box:

The height may also be outside the triangle, also represented by a dashed line and a 90-degree box:

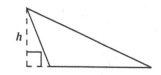

USING THE PYTHAGOREAN THEOREM

The *Pythagorean Theorem* states that you can find the length of any one side of a right triangle with the side lengths of the other two sides by using the formula $a^2 + b^2 = c^2$, where a and b are the shorter sides and c is the hypotenuse, opposite the 90-degree angle and the longest side of the triangle. Note that this theorem *only* works on a right triangle.

SAVING TIME WITH COMMON RIGHT TRIANGLES

Certain right triangles have commonly used side-length ratios, so before you place two side lengths into the Pythagorean, see whether it fits one of the ratios. Note that these triangles and ratios are in that pop-up Reference box on the digital test.

» **3:4:5 triangle.** In this triangle, the two shorter sides are 3 and 4 and the hypotenuse is 5.

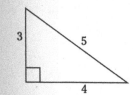

This is a ratio, so the side lengths can be any multiple of these numbers, including 6:8:10 (2 times 3:4:5) and 9:12:15 (3 times 3:4:5).

» **45-45-90 triangle, also known as an *isosceles right triangle*.** This is basically a square cut from corner to corner, resulting in two identical triangles with angles 45°, 45°, 90° and a side-length ratio of $1:1:\sqrt{2}$.

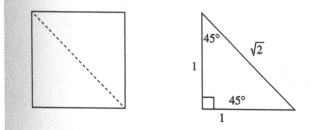

The side lengths of this triangle may appear as any multiple of this ratio, such as $5 : 5 : 5\sqrt{2}$.

» **30-60-90 triangle.** This is basically an equilateral triangle cut perfectly in half, resulting in mirrored triangles with angles $30°, 60°, 90°$ and a side-length ratio of $1 : 2 : \sqrt{3}$.

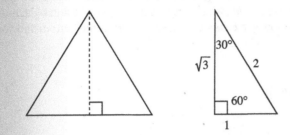

The 30-60-90 makes a regular appearance on the SAT. Just keep in mind that the hypotenuse is twice the length of the smallest side, and if you forget, it's right there in the Reference box. If a math question reads, "Given a 30-60-90 triangle of hypotenuse 20, find the area" or "Given a 30-60-90 triangle of hypotenuse 100, find the perimeter," you've got this because you can find the lengths of the other sides:

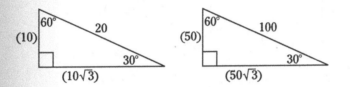

Also, if an SAT question asks for the height of an equilateral triangle, you can use the 30-60-90 triangle to solve it.

TIP

All right, enough talking . . . er, writing. Try these:

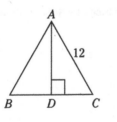

In this equilateral triangle, the length of segment AD is

PLAY

(A) 6

(B) 9

(C) $6\sqrt{2}$

(D) $6\sqrt{3}$

In the 30–60–90 triangle formed by *ABD*, the hypotenuse is 12 and the base is 6 because it's half the hypotenuse. Segment *AD* is the height, which is $6\sqrt{3}$, Choice (D), according to the ratio.

Triangles are among the most common math topics on the SAT, plus these concepts underlie other upcoming math topics, including trapezoids and trigonometry.

Drawing rectangles and squares

Of course, you know what rectangles and squares are. The SAT, being what it is, brings you this basic topic in some form that you haven't seen before. This book, being the remedy for the SAT, shows you what to expect and how to handle it. But first some basics:

» **A *quadrilateral* is any four-sided figure.** The sum of the angles of any quadrilateral is 360 degrees.

» **A *rectangle* is a quadrilateral with four right angles,** which makes the opposite sides equal. The area of a rectangle is *length × width*, where *length* is the longer side and *width* is the shorter side. The area can also be found with *base × height*, where *base* is the bottom and *height* is, well, height, regardless of which is longer.

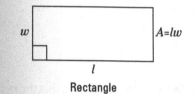

Rectangle

» **A *square* is a rectangle with four equal sides.** The area of a square is s^2, where s refers to a side length.

» **A *regular* shape is any shape having equal sides and angles.** For example, an equilateral triangle is a regular triangle, and a square is a regular quadrilateral.

Simple, right? Here's what the SAT does with it:

PLAY

In a certain rectangle, if the length and width were both reduced by 50%, how would the area of the rectangle change?

(A) The area would decrease by 25%.

(B) The area would decrease by 40%.

(C) The area would decrease by 50%.

(D) The area would decrease by 75%.

Draw a rectangle and give the side lengths simple numbers, preferably even ones since you'll be dividing them by half, such as 8×10, for an area of 80. Now perform said division by half, so the new side lengths are 4×5 for a new area of 20, which is a 75% decrease from the original area. The answer is Choice (D).

Drawing trapezoids and parallelograms

You know these shapes as well, but here's a review of how they work and how to manage them on the SAT.

» **A *parallelogram* is a quadrilateral where opposite sides and angles are equal, but the angles aren't necessarily right angles.** It's like a rectangle that got stepped on. The area of a parallelogram is *base* × *height*, where the *base* is the top or bottom (same thing) and the *height* is the *distance* between the two bases. As in a triangle, the height is represented by a dashed line with a right-angle box.

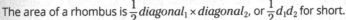

Parallelogram

» **A *rhombus* is a parallelogram with four equal sides.** It's like a square that also got stepped on. The rhombus is measured by the distance between the angles, known as *d* for *diagonal*. The area of a rhombus is $\frac{1}{2} diagonal_1 \times diagonal_2$, or $\frac{1}{2} d_1 d_2$ for short.

Rhombus

» A *trapezoid* is a quadrilateral with two sides that are parallel and two sides that are not. The area of a trapezoid is $\frac{1}{2}(base_1 + base_2) \times height$, or $\frac{1}{2}(b_1 + b_2)h$, where the bases are the two parallel sides, and the height is the distance between them. If you're not sure how to remember this, it's just base times height, but you average the bases first. Or you can check the graphic at the beginning of the Math Test.

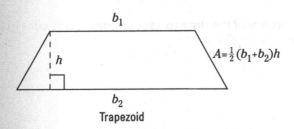

Trapezoid

» **Other polygons that you may see include the *pentagon*, the *hexagon*, and the *octagon*,** having five, six, and eight sides, respectively. If you have to measure the area, just cut these into smaller shapes. The SAT always gives you enough detail to solve the problem.

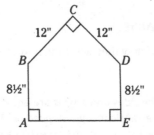

As shown in the diagram, an official major league home plate has the shape of a pentagon. Given the measurements shown, the area of this pentagon is

(A) $144 + 12\sqrt{2}$

(B) $96 + 12\sqrt{2}$

(C) $84 + 96\sqrt{2}$

(D) $72 + 102\sqrt{2}$

The secret is to split the pentagon into separate shapes, such as a triangle and a rectangle. Look at the triangle, BCD. Because angle C is a right angle, and the two sides adjacent to C are the same length, BCD is an isosceles right triangle, also known as a 45-45-90 triangle, with the side-length ratio $s : s : s\sqrt{2}$. Therefore, the hypotenuse BD is $12\sqrt{2}$, which is also the length of the rectangle. Now find the areas of these separate shapes and add them together.

The triangle's base and height are each 12. Sure, it's rotated, but that doesn't matter: $\frac{1}{2}(12)(12) = 72$. The rectangle has a base and height of $12\sqrt{2}$ and $8\frac{1}{2}$, respectively, which multiply to $\left(12\sqrt{2}\right)\left(8\frac{1}{2}\right) = 102\sqrt{2}$. Fortunately, that matches an answer: Choice (D). Note that the SAT doesn't make you calculate the exact answer.

Drawing circles

Of course, you know circles, but the SAT puts its own spin on these, too. Like everything else SAT, and so often repeated because it's always so true, any trick is easy for you to handle if you've seen the trick before. But first, some basics:

» **The *radius* goes from the center of the circle to its outer edge.** It's the same length no matter which point of the circle it touches.

Radius

» **Two *radii* (not in a line) create an isosceles triangle.** This makes sense because an isosceles triangle has two equal sides.

» **A *chord* is a line segment that joins any two points on the circumference of a circle.** The two points can range from close together to at opposite ends of the circle.

» **The *diameter* is a chord that goes through the *center* of the circle.** It's also twice the length of the radius.

Diameter

» **The *circumference* is the distance around the circle.** Find the circumference, C, by using either $C = 2\pi r$, where r is the radius, or $C = \pi d$, where d is the diameter, because the diameter is twice the radius.

Circumference

» ***Pi,*** **shown by the Greek letter π, is the ratio of the circumference to the diameter.** If you take the circumference of any circle and divide it by its diameter, the result is always approximately 3.14, represented by π.

» **Don't memorize the value of π.** Just know that it's slightly more than 3.

» **The *area* of a circle is $A = \pi r^2$.** If you forget any of these equations, click the Reference button at the top right of the digital Math Test.

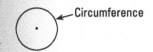

» **A *tangent* is a line or other shape that touches the circle at exactly one point.** The radius from the center of the circle to the point of tangency is perpendicular to the tangent.

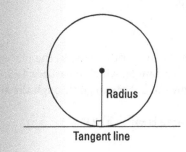

Radius

Tangent line

You know these concepts, and now you've refreshed how they work. The secret is to be fluid in converting one measure to another, such as a radius to circumference or area. Here's an SAT-style question on circles:

PLAY

The radius of circle A is twice the radius of circle B. How many times greater than the area of circle B is the area of circle A?

(A) Two times greater

(B) Three times greater

(C) Four times greater

(D) Six times greater

Pick a radius for circle A, such as 6. If that's twice the radius of circle B, then circle B has a radius of 3. Now find the areas. Place 6 and 3 for the radii of the two circles to find their areas: $\pi r^2 = \pi (6)^2 = 36\pi$ and $\pi r^2 = \pi (3)^2 = 9\pi$. Because 36π is four times greater than 9π, the answer is Choice (C).

It's a basic concept that the SAT turns sideways to throw you off. Of course, any question like this one is easy for you now.

Drawing overlapping shapes

The SAT places two shapes, with one overlapping the other, like a dinner plate on a placemat.

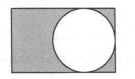

The SAT then asks you for the area of the placemat not covered by the dinner plate, or in SAT terms, the area of the shaded portion of the drawing. The way that you solve this is so simple that you need to try not to laugh out loud when you see this on the exam.

1. **Find the areas of the two shapes, separately.**

2. **Subtract the smaller area from the larger area.**

3. **Leave your answer in terms of π.**

The question gives you the numbers that you need to answer this one. In the placemat example, it tells you that the circle touches the edges of the rectangle, which measures 4×7. You can thus derive that the circle has a diameter of 4, for a radius of 2. Now to go through the steps:

1. **The rectangle area is $4 \times 7 = 28$ and the circle area is $\pi r^2 = \pi (2)^2 = 4\pi$.**

2. **Subtract the shapes for $28 - 4\pi$.**

3. **And you're done.**

You'll hardly ever have to calculate the actual value of 4π to subtract from 28. Instead, just pick $28 - 4\pi$ from the list of answers, stop laughing, and go on to the next question.

Overlapping shapes are somewhat common on the SAT Math, so make sure you have this topic down by practicing.

Drawing parts of circles

To draw part of a circle, just draw the whole circle and take the fraction of the circle. Here are the basics and the exact steps:

>> **An *arc* is part of the circumference,** like an *arch*. The degree measure of an arc is the same as its *central angle*, which originates at the center of the circle.

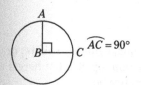

>> **A *sector* is part of the whole circle,** like a slice of pizza. The *arc* is the leftover crust of the pizza (if you don't eat it), and the *sector* is the slice itself. The degree measure of a sector is the same as that of an arc.

Here's how you find the length of an arc:

1. Find the circumference of the entire circle.

2. Put the degree measure of the arc over 360 and reduce the fraction.

3. Multiply the circumference by the fraction.

Here's how you find the area of a sector:

1. Find the area of the entire circle.

2. Put the degree measure of the sector over 360 and reduce the fraction.

3. Multiply the area by the fraction.

Finding the area of a sector is exactly like finding the length of an arc, except for that first step. Now try a couple:

PLAY

Find the length of minor arc *AC*.

(A) 36π

(B) 60

(C) 18π

(D) 6π

Start with the circumference of the whole circle: $2\pi r = 2\pi(18) = 36\pi$. Don't multiply 36π out. Next, put the degree measure of the arc over 360: $\frac{60°}{360°} = \frac{1}{6}$. Finally, multiply the circumference by the fraction: $36\pi \times \frac{1}{6} = 6\pi$, for answer Choice (D).

TIP

The *degree measure* of the arc is not the *length* of the arc. The length is always a portion of the circumference, typically with π in it. If you chose Choice (B) in this example, you found the degree measure instead of the length.

Parts of circles are fairly common on the SAT, so be sure you have this down, along with its variations.

Drawing 3-D shapes

Almost every SAT has a couple questions dealing with a box, cylinder, sphere, or cone. The equations for these 3-D shapes are included in the Reference pop-up box, but here's a review of what you need — because everyone forgets to check the Reference box.

Drawing rectangular solids and cubes

Any rectangular solid — also known as a *rectangular prism* — on the SAT is a perfect shoebox: Each side is a rectangle, and each corner is 90°. This keeps it easy.

>> **Volume of a rectangular solid:**

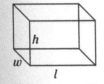

Rectangular solid

The same way that the area of a rectangle is *length* × *width*, the volume is the area multiplied by the height, for *length* × *width* × *height*, or $V = lwh$.

>> **Surface area of a rectangular solid:**

The official equation, where *l* is length, *w* is width, and *h* is height, is $2[(lw)+(lh)+(wh)]$. Have fun memorizing that one. Instead, *understand* it. A rectangular solid is six rectangles, so measure the surface area of each rectangle. The front and back are the same, so measure one and multiply by two. Same goes for the top and bottom and left side and right side. Fortunately, rectangular solid surface area questions are rare, so don't worry about that equation.

>> **Volume of a pyramid:**

A pyramid has a square base and four identical triangular sides. Like a rectangular solid, find the volume by multiplying the length, width, and height, but with a pyramid, you divide all this by 3: $\frac{1}{3}lwh$.

>> **Surface area of a pyramid:**

There is no sensible formula for finding the surface area of a pyramid, and fortunately these questions are practically nonexistent. If you do get one, you know what to do: Find the areas of each triangle and the square base, and add 'em up.

» Volume of a cube: $V = s^3$

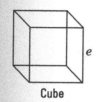

Cube

A cube is exactly like a rectangular solid, only the *length, width,* and *height* are the same, so they're called edges, or e. Technically, the volume of a cube is the same as that of a rectangular solid, *length × width × height*, but because they're all edges, it's *edge × edge × edge*, or e^3.

» Surface area of a cube:

Cube surface area questions are more common, and fortunately, simpler. Say a cube has an edge length of 2, so each side has an area of e^2, which in this case is 4 (because it's a square). With six sides, the surface area is 6×4, which is 24. This is also known as $6e^2$.

What's also common is that the SAT gives you the volume of a cube and asks you for the surface area, or vice versa. Whether you get the volume or the surface area, the secret is to backsolve and get the *edge*, then calculate what the question is asking.

PLAY

A certain cube has a volume of 27. What is its surface area?

If the volume is 27, backsolve this to get the edge:

$$e^3 = 27$$
$$e = 3$$

Now place the edge length of 3 into the surface area equation:

$$A = 6e^2$$
$$= 6(3)^2$$
$$= 54$$

And the surface area is 54.

The SAT, of course, contains variations on this theme, but they're all based on the same concept and just as easily learned.

Drawing cylinders and cones

You may be asked to find the volume of a cylinder or cone, but rarely the surface area. A question asking for the surface area also provides the surface area equation, and your task will simply be to place the numbers into the equation. The volume questions, however, are more common, and the equations are in the Reference pop-up box.

VOLUME OF A CYLINDER

Cylinder

A cylinder on the SAT is also called a *right circular cylinder,* where it's like a can of soda or an energy drink. Each base is a circle, and each angle is 90°. The volume of a cylinder is simply the area of the circle — one of its bases — times its height. The area of a circle is πr^2, times the height h, making the volume $\pi r^2 h$.

VOLUME OF A CONE

A cone has a circular base and sides that taper to a point. Its volume is the same as the cylinder, only divided by 3: $\frac{1}{3}\pi r^2 h$.

If a cylinder has a radius of 3 and a height of 4, you can place these into the equation and find its volume:

$$V = \pi r^2 h$$
$$= \pi (3)^2 4$$
$$= 36\pi$$

What's more common is that the SAT gives you the volume and radius and asks for the height, or it gives you the volume and height and asks for the radius. Either way, just take the numbers from the question and place them into the equation.

Drawing spheres

Like the cylinder and cone, most sphere questions ask for volume but rarely surface area. The volume equation is given in the beginning graphic, and the surface area equation, if needed, is given with the question.

A *sphere* is a perfectly round ball, like a basketball. Like a circle, it has a radius, so for its volume, simply place the radius into the equation: $\frac{4}{3}\pi r^3$.

Here's one to try:

PLAY

Which of the following is the volume of a sphere that has a radius of 3?

(A) 72π

(B) 54π

(C) 36π

(D) 18π

Place the radius into the volume equation. Remember, on the SAT, the math is simple:

$$V = \frac{4}{3}\pi r^3$$
$$= \frac{4}{3}\pi (3)^3$$
$$= \frac{4}{3}\pi 27$$
$$= 4\pi 9$$
$$= 36\pi$$

And the answer is Choice (C).

Sphere questions are like any other on the SAT Math Test: They look challenging but are simple to answer, especially with practice.

Solving trigonometry problems

Unlike the ACT, which typically has at least five trig questions among its 60 Math Test questions, the SAT usually has only one or two trig questions in its 44 Math Test questions. The scope of SAT trigonometry is also narrower, and this is a topic that you can move lower on your priority list. That said, if you got this far, you'll have no problem with these topics. This section covers what you need to know, even if you've never studied trigonometry.

Solving right triangles with SOH CAH TOA

SOH CAH TOA stands for

$$\text{Sine} = \frac{\text{Opposite}}{\text{Hypotenuse}}$$
$$\text{Cosine} = \frac{\text{Adjacent}}{\text{Hypotenuse}}$$
$$\text{Tangent} = \frac{\text{Opposite}}{\text{Adjacent}}$$

Opposite, adjacent, and *hypotenuse* refer to the sides of a right triangle in relation to one of the acute angles. For example, consider this right triangle:

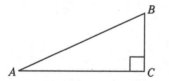

As you know, side *AB* is the *hypotenuse* (opposite the right angle and the longest side of the right triangle). For angle *A*, side *BC* is *opposite*, and side *AC* is *adjacent*. For angle *B*, they switch: Side *AC* is opposite, and side *BC* is adjacent.

Use SOH CAH TOA to quickly find the sine, cosine, or tangent of any acute angle in the right triangle.

» **To find sin A (the sine of angle A), use the SOH part of SOH CAH TOA.** Place the length of the side opposite angle A (in this case, side BC) over the hypotenuse (side AB).

$$\sin A = \frac{\text{Opposite}}{\text{Hypotenuse}}$$

$$\sin A = \frac{\overline{BC}}{\overline{AB}}$$

» **To find cos A (the cosine of angle A), use the CAH part of SOH CAH TOA.** Place the length of the side adjacent to angle A (in this case, side AC) over the hypotenuse (side AB).

$$\cos A = \frac{\text{Adjacent}}{\text{Hypotenuse}}$$

$$\cos A = \frac{\overline{AC}}{\overline{AB}}$$

» **To find tan A (the tangent of angle A), use the TOA part of SOH CAH TOA.** Place the length of the side opposite angle A over the side adjacent to angle A.

$$\tan A = \frac{\text{Opposite}}{\text{Adjacent}}$$

$$\tan A = \frac{\overline{BC}}{\overline{AC}}$$

SOH CAH TOA only works with a *right triangle* and only with an *acute angle*, not the right angle.

TIP

Because sine and cosine are always a shorter side over the longer hypotenuse, sine and cosine can never be greater than 1. Tangent, however, can be greater than 1. You don't need to know the common values of sine and cosine, but these can be handy:

» $\sin 90° = 1$ and $\sin 0° = 0$

» $\cos 90° = 0$ and $\cos 0° = 1$

Find the sine of angle A in this right triangle:

PLAY

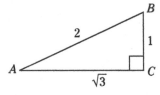

(A) 2

(B) $\sqrt{3}$

(C) 1

(D) $\frac{1}{2}$

Using the SOH in SOH CAH TOA, you know that the sine of angle A comes from the opposite (1) over the hypotenuse (2), for an answer of $\frac{1}{2}$, which matches Choice (D).

Three additional ratios appear less frequently than sine, cosine, and tangent but are just as easy to find. These are cosecant (csc), secant (sec), and cotangent (cot). Basically, you find the sine, cosine, or tangent and take the reciprocal to find cosecant, secant, or cotangent. The angle is usually represented by the Greek letter theta, θ:

$$\csc \theta = \frac{1}{\sin \theta}$$

$$\sec \theta = \frac{1}{\cos \theta}$$

$$\cot \theta = \frac{1}{\cot \theta}$$

TIP

If you get mixed up as to whether cosecant or secant is the reciprocal of sine or cosine, just remember this tip: *C* in *cosecant* goes with *S* in *sine*. *S* in *secant* goes with *C* in *cosine*.

Here's another:

PLAY

For this right triangle, if $\tan B = \frac{4}{3}$, find $\cos A$.

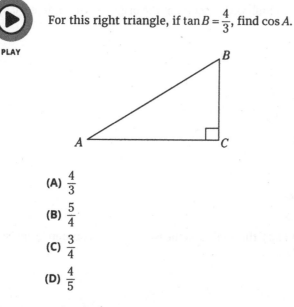

(A) $\frac{4}{3}$

(B) $\frac{5}{4}$

(C) $\frac{3}{4}$

(D) $\frac{4}{5}$

If $\tan B = \frac{4}{3}$ and tangent is opposite over adjacent (the TOA from SOH CAH TOA), then draw the triangle like this:

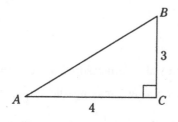

Spotting this as one of the common right triangles, you automatically throw down 5 for the hypotenuse instead of using the Pythagorean Theorem.

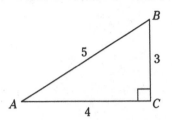

Cosine is CAH, which is adjacent over hypotenuse. Therefore, $\cos A = \frac{4}{5}$, which matches Choice (D).

Solving unit circles and radians

The *unit circle* is a circle drawn on the x–y graph with a center at the origin — coordinates $(0,0)$ — and a radius of 1.

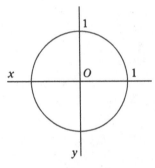

Starting with the radius of the circle at $(1,0)$, the angle θ is measured going counterclockwise.

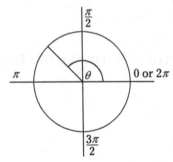

In this drawing, $\theta = 135°$. However, the angle isn't always measured in degrees; rather, it's in *radians*, which means that it's in terms of π, where $\pi = 180°$, making $135° = \frac{3\pi}{4}$.

An angle measuring 45° also measures $\frac{\pi}{4}$ radians. An angle measuring 270° also measures $\frac{3\pi}{2}$ radians. More importantly, or the way it's used on the SAT, you can tell which quadrant an angle is in from the range of radians. In other words, an angle between $\frac{\pi}{2}$ and π is in the second quadrant. For the angle θ,

» $0 < \theta < \frac{\pi}{2}$ places the angle in the first quadrant.

» $\frac{\pi}{2} < \theta < \pi$ places the angle in the second quadrant.

>> $\pi < \theta < \frac{3\pi}{2}$ places the angle in the third quadrant.

>> $\frac{3\pi}{2} < \theta < 2\pi$ places the angle in the fourth quadrant.

When SOH CAH TOA is applied to an angle in the unit circle, it's always for the angle θ, which comes from the radius of the circle. The *hypotenuse* is this radius, the *adjacent* is the x-value, and the *opposite* is the y-value. Consider this example, where $\theta = 60°$ and the radius meets the circle at $\left(\frac{1}{2}, \sqrt{3}\right)$, where on the xy graph, $x = \frac{1}{2}$ and $y = \sqrt{3}$.

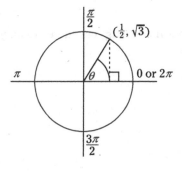

The sine of θ is the opposite over the hypotenuse, which in this case is $\frac{\sqrt{3}}{2}$. The cosine of θ is the adjacent over the hypotenuse, $\frac{0.5}{1}$, or $\frac{1}{2}$. The tangent of θ is the opposite over the adjacent, which is $\frac{\sqrt{3}}{1}$, or $\sqrt{3}$.

Knowing the quadrant and the sine, cosine, or tangent of an angle on the unit circle, you can find exactly where the angle is and solve almost any problem about it.

PLAY

If $\frac{\pi}{2} < \theta < \pi$ and $\cos\theta = -\frac{3}{5}$, what is $\sin\theta$?

(A) $-\frac{4}{5}$

(B) $-\frac{3}{5}$

(C) $\frac{3}{5}$

(D) $\frac{4}{5}$

The first expression, $\frac{\pi}{2} < \theta < \pi$, places the angle in the second quadrant, and $\cos\theta = -\frac{3}{5}$ means the ratio of the x-value of the endpoint to the radius is $-\frac{3}{5}$. Because the hypotenuse (or radius) is always positive, the x-value is negative. The $\sin\theta$, being the opposite over hypotenuse, is therefore $\frac{4}{5}$, and the correct answer is Choice (D).

To convert from π radians to degrees, remove the π and multiply by 180:
$$\pi = 180°$$
$$3\pi = 520°$$

And, to convert from degrees to π radians, do the opposite: Divide by 180 and place the π:

$$360° = 2\pi$$
$$90° = \frac{\pi}{2}$$

Use that to answer this question:

PLAY

If an engine rotates 1,800 degrees per second, what is its rotation per second in π radians?

(A) 8π

(B) 10π

(C) 12π

(D) 14π

Convert the 1,800 degrees to π radians by dividing by 180 and placing π:

$1,800° \div 180° = 10 \rightarrow 10\pi$ for Choice (B).

Solving trigonometric equations

You see many more of these equations in Algebra II and Trig, but there are only a few that you need on the SAT. Try these on this right triangle:

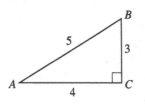

1. $\dfrac{\sin x}{\cos x} = \tan x$

    Take angle A, for example. Using SOH CAH TOA, you know that $\sin A = \frac{3}{5}$, $\cos A = \frac{4}{5}$, and $\tan A = \frac{3}{4}$.

    Now prove this equation by placing these values:

    $$\frac{\sin x}{\cos x} = \tan x$$
    $$\frac{\frac{3}{5}}{\frac{4}{5}} = \frac{3}{5} \times \frac{5}{4} = \frac{3}{4}$$

2. $\sin x = \cos(90 - x)$ or $\sin A = \cos B$

    Remember, the two non-right angles total 90°, so 90° minus one angle equals the other angle. With the triangle above, $\sin A = \frac{3}{5}$ equals $\cos B = \frac{3}{5}$.

3. $\sin^2 x + \cos^2 x = 1$

    Back to the 3-4-5 triangle above. $\sin A = \frac{3}{5}$ and $\cos A = \frac{4}{5}$. First square these: $\sin^2 A = \left(\frac{3}{5}\right)^2 = \frac{9}{25}$ and $\cos^2 A = \left(\frac{4}{5}\right)^2 = \frac{16}{25}$. Now add them: $\frac{9}{25} + \frac{16}{25} = \frac{25}{25} = 1$.

The SAT asks these in a conceptual form. If you understand these three equations, and more importantly, *recognize* them in the question, you save yourself a lot of math and give yourself a lot of laughter as you answer the question in well under a minute. Try this one:

PLAY

If $\cos a° = n$, which of the following must be true for all values of a?

(A) $\sin^2 a = n$

(B) $\cos(90-a)° = n$

(C) $\sin(90-a)° = n$

(D) $\tan(90-a)° = n$

Knowing that $\sin x = \cos(90-x)$, because you just read it a second ago, you know that $\cos a° = \sin(90-a)°$. Because these each equal n, the answer is Choice (C).

See? Almost no math. Practice these concepts and learn to recognize them *quickly*.

Measuring Statistics and Probability

The topic of statistics and probability builds upon numbers and operations covered in the earlier section "Simplifying Numbers and Operations." Like every other topic in SAT Math, the numeric part is always simple, and knowing how to set up the solution is key. This section reviews SAT-style questions on sets-of-number topics that include averages (also known as arithmetic mean), median, mode, and range, along with probability and reading graphs.

Measuring the mean, median, and mode

Of all the methods to quantify or measure a set of numbers or data, the most common — and what you see on the SAT — involves the *mean, median,* and *mode*. Your job is to look past the tricky way that the SAT sets up the question and find the simple underlying concept.

Measuring the mean

Sometimes the SAT gives you a group of numbers and asks for the *average* (also called the *mean* or *arithmetic mean*). To find the average, just total up the numbers and divide that by the count of numbers you just added. For example, to find the average of 2, 4, and 9, add those numbers and divide by 3, because there are three numbers. It looks like this:

$$a = \frac{2+4+9}{3}$$
$$= \frac{15}{3}$$
$$= 5$$

If you have the average and *some* of the numbers, set up the equation with x as the missing number. If the average of 3, 6, 14, and some unknown number is 7, use x as the unknown number:

$$7 = \frac{3+6+14+x}{4}$$
$$7 = \frac{23+x}{4}$$
$$28 = 23+x$$
$$x = 5$$

This type of question usually looks like this:

PLAY

Aisha has taken three tests, with an average (arithmetic mean) of 88. What grade must she receive on her next test for an overall average of 90 to get her A?

(A) 90

(B) 94

(C) 96

(D) 98

Set up the equation with x as the upcoming test. You don't know the other three test scores, but you do know they average 88, so use 88 for each one:

$$90 = \frac{88 + 88 + 88 + x}{4}$$
$$90 = \frac{264 + x}{4}$$
$$360 = 264 + x$$
$$x = 96$$

Aisha needs 96 on this next test for that A. She'll get it. The correct answer is Choice (C).

Measuring the median and mode

The *median* is the middle number in a list, when the list is in numerical order. Say you have the numbers 5, 3, 8, 7, 2 and need the median. Put the numbers in order, 2, 3, 5, 7, 8, and the middle number, or median, is 5.

If there are two middle numbers (say with 2, 4, 5, 7, 8, 10), average the two middle numbers. In this example, the two middle numbers are 5 and 7, so the median is 6.

Finally there's the *mode*. In a mixed bag of numbers, the *mode* is the number or numbers that pop up most frequently. So with the numbers 3, 4, 4, 5, 8, 8, 9, there are two modes, 4 and 8. You can also have a set with no mode at all if everything shows up the same number of times, as with 3, 4, 5, 6.

PLAY

Andrew has a median score of 83 on five tests. If he scores 97 and 62 on his next two tests, his median score will

(A) increase to 90

(B) decrease to 82

(C) decrease to 79.5

(D) remain the same

The median is the score in the middle. If 83 is in the middle, placing 97 on one side and 62 on the other doesn't change the middle number. The correct answer is Choice (D).

Once again, the SAT takes a topic you know fairly well and introduces variations that may throw you the first time you see them.

Measuring the range

The *range* is the distance between the lowest and highest numbers. For example, if your lowest exam score is 82 and your highest is 110, because you got those bonus questions, the range is the difference between those scores: $110 - 82 = 28$.

The SAT doesn't make it that simple, but this book makes it that easy. On the SAT, the range represents something like sales tax, units per box, or something that you somehow have to calculate. So all you do is calculate it, and the answer is easy.

For example, if each volleyball team has either 4 or 6 players, and there are 12 teams at the tournament, what are the *lowest* and *highest* possible numbers of players? For the lowest number, use 4 players per each of the 12 teams: $4 \times 12 = 48$. For the highest number, use 6 per team: $6 \times 12 = 72$.

Try this one:

PLAY

Mariama places between $\frac{1}{5}$ and $\frac{1}{4}$, inclusive, of her weekly paycheck into a savings account. If she placed \$150 into her savings account last week, then how much, in dollars, *could* last week's paycheck have been? Disregard the dollar sign when writing your answer.

First, find the amount of her paycheck with \$150 as $\frac{1}{4}$ of it:

$$\frac{1}{4}x = \$150$$
$$x = \$600$$

Then find the amount of her paycheck with \$150 as $\frac{1}{5}$ of it:

$$\frac{1}{5}x = \$150$$
$$x = \$750$$

So her paycheck was between \$600 and \$750. Don't worry about the dollar sign, so any number you place between 600 and 750 (including those numbers because the question states *inclusive*) is considered correct.

Measuring probability

The *probability* of an event means how likely it is to occur. A 50 percent chance of rain means that the probability of rain is $\frac{1}{2}$. A probability can be defined as a fraction, percent, or decimal. Here's the equation for the probability of an event, represented by the letter *e*.

$$\text{probability } (p_e) = \frac{\text{the number you want}}{\text{the number possible}}$$

Say that you have a jar of 18 marbles where 7 are blue. The probability of reaching in and grabbing a blue marble is $\frac{7}{18}$, because there are 7 that you want and 18 possible.

Probability is always between 0 and 1. If something will *definitely* happen, the probability is 1, or 100 percent. The probability that the sun will rise tomorrow is 100 percent. If something will definitely *not* happen, the probability is 0. The probability that Elvis will sing again is 0.

The probabilities of different outcomes where only one can happen always add up to 1. Say you take a history exam. Say also the probability of you getting an A is 60 percent, a B is 20 percent, a C is 10 percent, a D is 5 percent, and an F is 5 percent. There's only one possible outcome — you can't get two grades on one exam — and all the probabilities add up to 100 percent.

If there are two events, and you want the probability of one *or* the other, add the probabilities. For that history exam, your probability of earning an A *or* a B is 80 percent, which comes from adding the 60 percent probability of an A to the 20 percent probability of a B.

If there are two *separate* events, and you want the probability of *both* happening, multiply the probabilities. Here's an example:

PLAY

Jenny arranges interviews with three potential employers. If each employer has a 50 percent probability of offering her a job, what's the probability that she gets offered all three?

(A) 10%

(B) 12.5%

(C) 75%

(D) 100%

These are three separate events, each with a probability of 50 percent. The probability of Jenny being offered all three jobs is $50\% \times 50\% \times 50\%$, or $\frac{1}{2} \times \frac{1}{2} \times \frac{1}{2} = \frac{1}{8}$, which calculates to 12.5% for Choice (B).

TIP

Probability questions are lower on the list of common SAT Math questions, but they do appear, and they're simple enough if you've worked a few.

Measuring graph data

Here are the three most common types of graphs you're likely to see on the SAT:

» Bar graph

» Circle or pie graph

» Two-axes line graph

Measuring bar graphs

A *bar graph* has vertical or horizontal bars.

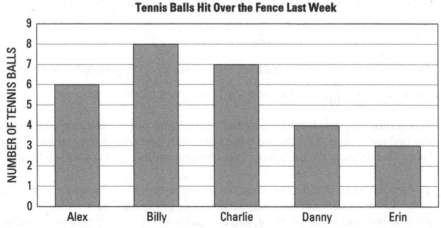

Measuring circle or pie charts

A *circle* or *pie chart* represents the total, or 100 percent.

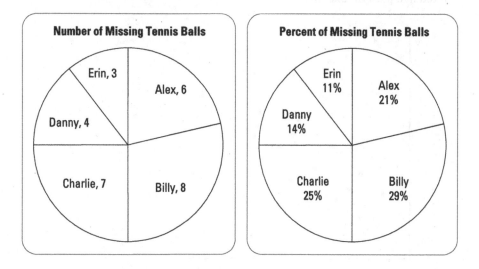

Measuring line graphs

A typical *line graph* has a bottom and a side axis.

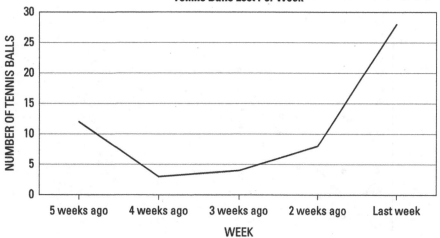

Measuring scatter plots

A special kind of two-axes graph is the *scatter plot*. A scatter plot contains a bunch of dots scattered in a pattern, like this:

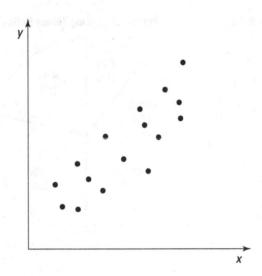

Notice how the points in this example seem to follow a certain flow, going up and to the right. When you see this, you can draw a line that captures the flow. This line is known as a *trend line* or *correlation*. On the test, you may be given a scatter plot and have to estimate where the points are going based on the trend line, like this:

On the SAT, a correlation is typically *linear*. Going left to right, if the correlation goes *up*, it's positive, and if it goes *down*, it's negative, just like the slope of a graphed line.

Which of the following best describes the data set?

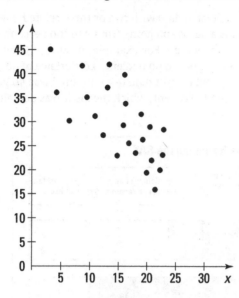

(A) A positive correlation

(B) A negative correlation

(C) An exponential correlation

(D) No correlation

There is clearly a correlation, which is rarely exponential (on the SAT), so out go Choices (C) and (D). Add the trend line to see whether the correlation is positive or negative:

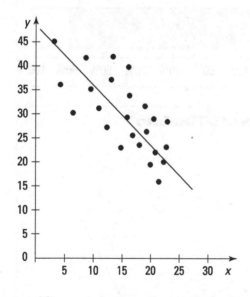

The trend line goes down, so the correlation is negative. Choice (B) it is.

Measuring multiple graphs

Sometimes the SAT places two graphs of related data with two or three related questions on these graphs. In this example, the first graph is a bar graph going from 0 to 100 percent. Read the graph by subtracting to find the appropriate percentage. For example, in 2016, "Grandparents won't donate a building" begins at 20 percent and goes to 50 percent, a difference of 30 percent. You've fallen into a trap if you say that "Grandparents won't donate a building" was 50 percent. In 2019, "Just felt like it" goes from 80 percent to 100 percent, which means it was actually 20 percent.

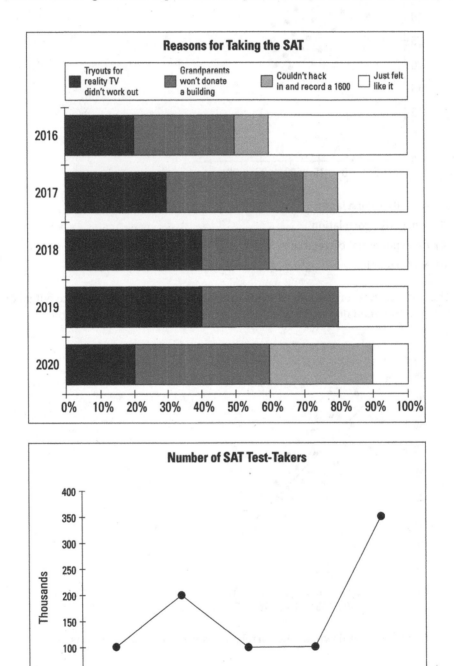

The second graph gives you the number of SAT test-takers in thousands. (By the way, these aren't real numbers.) Be sure to look at the labels of the axes. For example, *Thousands* along the side axis tells you that in 2020, there weren't 350 test-takers but 350,000. Using the two graphs together, you can find out the number of test-takers who took the SAT for a particular reason. For example, in 2017, 200,000 students took the test. Also in 2017, "Couldn't hack in and record a 1600" (from 70 to 80, or 10 percent) made up 10 percent of the reasons for taking the SAT. Multiply 10 percent or $0.10 \times 200,000 = 20,000$ test-takers.

The SAT may feature two or three questions about a particular graph or set of graphs. When you encounter these, start with the question, then go to the graphs. Answer the following question based on the two preceding practice graphs:

PLAY

The number of students who took the SAT in 2020 because their grandparents wouldn't donate a building was how much greater than the number of students who took the SAT in 2018 because they couldn't hack in and record a 1600?

(A) 250,000

(B) 140,000

(C) 120,000

(D) 100,000

In 2020, "Grandparents won't donate a building" accounted for 40 percent of test-taking reasons (from 20 to 60). Because 2020 had 350,000 test-takers, multiply $0.40 \times 350,000 = 140,000$. In 2018, "Couldn't hack in and record a 1600" counted for 20 percent of test-taking reasons (60 to 80). In 2018, 100,000 students took the test. Multiply $0.20 \times 100,000 = 20,000$. The correct answer is $140,000 - 20,000 = 120,000$, or Choice (C).

Block 4

Taking a (Shortened) Practice Test

You're now ready to take a shortened practice SAT. The following practice exam consists of 28 Reading and Writing questions (split into two 14-question modules) along with 22 Math questions (split into two 11-question modules), for 50 questions total.

You get 17 minutes for each Reading and Writing module and 18 minutes for each Math module. Those plus the 2-minute break between modules and the 10-minute break between sections bring the exam to just under one and a half hours. No answer sheet is provided, so circle your answer selection right here in this book.

Take this practice test under normal exam conditions and approach it as you would the real SAT:

>> **Work where you won't be interrupted.** Leave your cell phone in another room, and ask anyone living with you (parents, siblings, dog) not to disturb you for the next few hours. (Good luck with that.)

>> **Practice with someone else who is taking the SAT.** This allows you to get used to the feeling of working with another person in the room; plus, this person can keep you focused and provide a sense of competition.

>> **Answer as many questions as time allows.** Consider answering all the easier questions within each section first and then going back to the harder questions. Because you're not penalized for guessing, go ahead and guess on the remaining questions before time expires.

>> **Set a timer for each section.** If you have time left at the end, review your answers (within the section), continue and finish your test early, or pause and catch your mental breath before moving on to the next section.

>> **Take breaks between sections.** Take two minutes after each module and ten minutes after the second Reading and Writing section.

>> **Work through the entire exam.** Get used to the experience of going through the entire exam in one sitting. Completing this shortened exam in a single sitting is good practice and will help you build endurance gradually in preparation for the full-length exam.

>> **Circle any question that you weren't sure of or that took too long.** If you took longer than a minute on any one question, or had to guess, you should brush up on that topic or strategy. After the exam, you naturally review the explanations for wrong answers, but this way you review the explanations for right answers that you had guessed on or could've found faster.

After completing this practice test, check your answers at the end of this block. You could review the explanations for *each* question, not just the ones you miss, but at least review the questions you missed along with those that you circled. The answer explanations provide insight and a review of everything from the previous blocks.

Ready? Grab a pencil, some scratch paper, a calculator, and a timer. Sit back, relax, and enjoy your trip through this abridged practice exam. Remember, you got this.

Section 1: Reading and Writing
Module 1

TIME: 17 minutes for 14 questions.

DIRECTIONS: Read these passages and answer the questions that follow based on what is stated or implied in the passages and accompanying diagrams, charts, or graphs. Each question has one best answer.

1. Modern communication has evolved to the point that door-to-door mail delivery is practically _____; that is, as out-of-date as having your mail delivered today by a mailman in a horse-drawn cart.

   Which choice completes the text with the most logical and precise word or phrase?

   (A) practical

   (B) unexpected

   (C) obsolete

   (D) insular

2. Loss of forested areas poses an increasing threat to the integrity of the nation's natural resources. As these areas are fragmented and disappear, so do the benefits they provide. By providing economic incentives to landowners to keep their forests as forests, we can _____ sustainable forest management and support strong markets for forest products.

   Which choice completes the text with the most logical and precise word or phrase?

   (A) access

   (B) determine

   (C) enrich

   (D) encourage

3. American bison once numbered 60 million in North America, with the population anchored in what is now the central United States. Many Indigenous cultures, especially in areas where the species was most abundant, developed strong ties with bison and relied upon them for sustenance, shelter, and cultural and religious practices. In the 19th century, bison were nearly driven to extinction through uncontrolled hunting and a U.S. policy of eradication tied to intentional harm against and control of Tribes. By 1889, only a few hundred wild bison remained. The _____ of bison contributed to the decline of healthy grassland ecosystems and, eventually, to the Dust Bowl in the 1930s.

   Which choice completes the text with the most logical and precise word or phrase?

   (A) persecution

   (B) enhancement

   (C) identification

   (D) persistence

4. The following text is an excerpt from *Daughter of the Sky: The Story of Amelia Earhart* by Paul L. Briand Jr. (1960). In this scene, Amelia Earhart, formerly a social worker, is being interviewed to be the first woman to fly across the Atlantic.

The demure Boston social worker survived the examination. Recalling the experience, Amelia said later: "I found myself in a curious situation. If they did not like me at all or found me wanting in too many respects, I would be deprived of the trip. If they liked me too well, they might be loath to drown me. It was, therefore, necessary for me to maintain an attitude of impenetrable mediocrity. Apparently I did, because I was chosen."

To what quality does Amelia Earhart attribute her success in the interview?

(A) her blazing courage

(B) her innate curiosity

(C) her opaque ordinariness

(D) her demure respectfulness

5. The following excerpt contains the concluding lines from Sonnet 73 by William Shakespeare. The speaker of the poem directly addresses someone he loves.

In me thou see'st the glowing of such fire,
That on the ashes of his youth doth lie
As the deathbed whereon it must expire,
Consumed with that which it was nourished by.
This thou perceivest, which makes thy love more strong.
To love that well which thou must leave ere long.

Which of the following best expresses the speaker's claim about his lover's reaction to his words?

(A) You see that I will soon die, and that understanding makes you love me more.

(B) You will be quickly consumed by the fires of passion and will cease to love me.

(C) Your love for me will fade away and die when I am no longer in your presence.

(D) Your youth prevents you from understanding the significance of true love and you will leave me.

6. Secretary of the Interior Deb Haaland made history by becoming the first Native American to serve as a U.S. cabinet secretary. Her life story is a legacy of firsts. After running for New Mexico Lieutenant Governor in 2014, Secretary Haaland became the first Native American woman to be elected to lead a state party. She is one of the first Native American women to serve in Congress and her family has a history of public service: Her father served as a 30-year combat Marine, and her mother is a Navy veteran who served as a federal employee for 25 years at the Bureau of Indian Affairs.

Which choice concludes the paragraph most effectively?

(A) At the age of 28, Haaland enrolled at the University of New Mexico (UNM) where she earned a Bachelor's degree in English and later earned her J.D. from UNM Law School.

(B) Secretary Haaland grew up in a military family; her father was a 30-year combat Marine, and, as a military child, she attended 13 public schools before graduating from Highland High School in Albuquerque.

(C) Secretary Haaland ran her own small business producing and canning Pueblo Salsa, served as a tribal administrator at San Felipe Pueblo, and became the first woman elected to the Laguna Development Corporation Board of Directors.

(D) As a 35th-generation New Mexican and member of the Pueblo of Laguna, Secretary Haaland has broken barriers and her achievements have opened the doors of opportunity for future generations.

7. The following excerpt is from *O Pioneers!* By Willa Cather (1913).

Of all the bewildering things about a new country, the absence of human landmarks is one of the most depressing and disheartening. The houses were small and were usually tucked away in low places; you did not see them until you came directly upon them. Most of them were built of the sod itself, and were only the inescapable ground in another form. The roads were but faint tracks in the grass, and the fields were scarcely noticeable. The record of the plow was insignificant, like the feeble scratches on stone left by prehistoric races, so indeterminate that they may, after all, be only the markings of glaciers, and not a record of human strivings.

The comparison between the plowed fields and "the feeble scratches on stone left by prehistoric races" serves which of the following functions in the text?

(A) To introduce the idea of human weakness

(B) To show that this settlement has a long history

(C) To describe the effects of glaciers

(D) To emphasize the primitive quality of the farming

8. About a century ago, in August 1914, what participants called "The Great War" and, ironically, "The War to End All Wars," _____. We know this conflict as World War I, one of the bloodiest periods in human history. When it ended in 1918, about 9 million soldiers were dead and the health of 7 million more was permanently disabled.

Which choice completes the text so that it conforms to the conventions of Standard English?

(A) begun

(B) had began

(C) has begun

(D) had begun

9. In 1859, Thomas Austin, an Australian who enjoyed hunting, released 24 rabbits on his land. The hunter stated that "introduction of a few rabbits could do little harm" and "might provide a touch of home." He liked to hunt. Before this time, _____ some domestic rabbits in Australia, mostly in cages or other enclosures. With a moderate climate, the wild rabbits bred all year round. Soon Australia had a rabbit problem with more than 200 million rabbits overrunning the land.

Which choice completes the text so that it conforms to the conventions of Standard English?

(A) there were

(B) there was

(C) their were

(D) they're was

10. The following text is adapted from *Crime Its Causes and Treatment* by Clarence Darrow (1922).

Strictly speaking, a crime is an act forbidden by the law of the land, and one which is considered sufficiently serious to warrant providing penalties for its commission. It does not necessarily follow that this act is either good _____ punishment follows for the violation of the law and not necessarily for any moral transgression.

Which choice completes the text so that it conforms to the conventions of Standard English?

(A) or bad; the

(B) or bad, the

(C) nor bad when

(D) nor bad because the

GO ON TO NEXT PAGE ▶

11. The NASA Juno mission, launched in August of 2011, was expected to arrive at its destination in July of 2016. The mission had a far-seeking _____ to the planet Jupiter to uncover the secrets of its origin and to search for evidence of water and ammonia.

Which choice completes the text so that it conforms to the conventions of Standard English?

(A) goal: to travel

(B) goal, to travel

(C) goal; to travel

(D) goal. To travel

12. Architect I. M. Pei is celebrated for his brilliant designs that have become attractions in cities around the world. He has designed such famous buildings as the John F. Kennedy Library in Boston, the Bank of China Tower in Hong Kong, and the Museum of Islamic Art in Qatar. His design for the main entrance to the Louvre, with _____ iconic glass and steel pyramid, has become a Parisian landmark.

Which choice completes the text so that it conforms to the conventions of Standard English?

(A) their

(B) it's

(C) its'

(D) its

13. The great Persian Empire extended from the shores of the Mediterranean to the east, far beyond the knowledge of the Greeks. _____ knowledge of the interior of Asia was very imperfect, and Alexander's expedition was rather that of an explorer than of a conqueror. How he overthrew the Persians and subdued an area as large as Europe in the space of twelve years reads like a romance rather than fact.

Which of the following completes the text with the most logical transition?

(A) However, their

(B) Indeed, their

(C) In contrast, their

(D) On the other hand, their

14. While researching a topic, a student has taken the following notes:

- Women have traditionally been caregivers but were prohibited from professionally practicing medicine until recent times.

- In Medieval times, women had limited roles as healers; Hildegard of Bingen was the most notable of Medieval healers.

- In 1849, Elizabeth Blackwell was the first woman to receive a medical degree from a U.S. university after being rejected from every medical school in the country except Geneva Medical College in New York.

- While the male students first thought Blackwell's application was a joke, they ultimately were impressed by her fierce dedication and supported her inclusion in their class.

- Blackwell founded the New York Infirmary for Indigent Women and Children, where she trained other women to become nurses and doctors.

The student wants to emphasize the distinguishing qualities of Elizabeth Blackwell. Which choice most effectively accomplishes this goal?

(A) Although she lived in Medieval times, Hildegard of Bingen was a trailblazer who created a path for Elizabeth Blackwell to follow.

(B) Without the intervention of the males in her medical school class at Geneva Medical College, Elizabeth Blackwell would never have become the first female physician in the U.S.

(C) Following a path first blazed by Hildegard of Bingen, Elizabeth Blackwell overcame gender discrimination with courage and determination and established the place of women as professional healthcare providers.

(D) By admitting Elizabeth Blackwell, Geneva Medical College took the first steps toward establishing a place for women in the practice of medicine.

Check Your Work.

Continue to the next module when you're ready to move on.

Module 2

TIME: 17 minutes for 14 questions.

DIRECTIONS: Read these passages and answer the questions that follow based on what is stated or implied in the passages and accompanying diagrams, charts, or graphs. Each question has one best answer.

1. In their various industries, the Egyptians made use of gold, silver, bronze, metallic iron, and copper, and their oxides, manganese, cobalt, alum, cinnabar, indigo, madder, brass, white lead, and lampblack. There is clear evidence that they smelted iron ore as early as 3400 B.C.E., maintaining a blast by means of leather tread-bellows. They also _____ temper the metal, and to make helmets, swords, lance-points, ploughs, tools, and other implements of iron.

Which choice completes the text with the most logical and precise word?

(A) refused to

(B) were reluctant to

(C) contrived to

(D) grew to

2. The Streamflow Monitoring Using Computer Vision Machine Learning project will develop a lower-cost method to quantify streamflow that can be used by states, tribes, and other organizations. This approach can supplement the current methods — that is, deployment of hydrological measurement equipment (stream gauges) that is costly and _____ specialized expertise. This user-friendly alternative relies on continuous photo imagery and machine learning to estimate streamflow.

Which choice completes the text with the most logical and precise word?

(A) requires

(B) prefers

(C) portrays

(D) predicts

3. The following is an excerpt from Charles Darwin's *On the Origin of Species* (1859).

A struggle for existence inevitably follows from the high rate at which all organic beings tend to increase. Every being, which during its natural lifetime produces several eggs or seeds, must suffer destruction during some period of its life, and during some season or occasional year; otherwise, on the principle of geometrical increase, its numbers would quickly become so inordinately great that no country could support the product. Hence, as more individuals are produced than can possibly survive, there must in every case be a struggle for existence, either one individual with another of the same species, or with the individuals of distinct species, or with the physical conditions of life.

Which choice best describes the function of the underlined portion in the text as a whole?

(A) It gives a specific example to support the generalization in the first sentence.

(B) It posits a new idea to counter a previously accepted conclusion.

(C) It provides further details about the particular species referred to earlier in the text.

(D) It draws a logical conclusion from the information in the previous sentences.

 GO ON TO NEXT PAGE

4. Non-native species are plants and animals living in areas where they do not naturally exist. "Non-native species" and "invasive species" cannot be used interchangeably. <u>Many commonly grown fruits and vegetables are not native to the U.S.</u> For example, tomatoes and hot peppers originated from South America, while lettuce was first grown by the Egyptians. Domestic cows are non-native to North America and were introduced as a food source and considered to be a beneficial organism in an agricultural setting.

Which choice best describes the function of the underlined portion in the text as a whole?

(A) It clarifies by elaborating on terms used in the previous sentence.

(B) It offers a specific example of a fruit and vegetable to support the generalization in the previous sentence.

(C) It notes an exception to the terms used in the previous sentence.

(D) It presents a counterclaim to the assertion in the first sentence.

5.

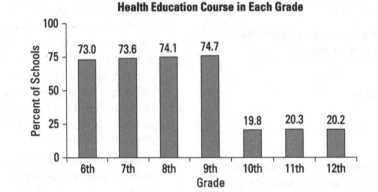

Percent of Schools That Taught a Required Health Education Course in Each Grade

Concerned about lack of awareness of certain health issues among students in the school system, the City School Superintendent decided to track the number of schools that provided health education in each grade of secondary school. Based on the data in the graph above, he concluded that most schools in the district were consistently providing a health education course in all grades of secondary school.

Which choice describes data that weakens the Superintendent's conclusion?

(A) All schools offered students some health education in every grade from 6 through 12.

(B) Fewer schools offered students in grades 10 through 12 a health education course than they offered students in grades 6 through 9.

(C) More schools offered students a health education course in grade 9 than in grade 6.

(D) No schools offered a health education course to students in grades 1 through 5.

6. Veterinarians who study animal behavior have entered a relatively new area of study. In earlier times, what was going on inside an animal's mind was not a concern. The Greek philosopher Aristotle (384–322 B.C.E.) said that animals couldn't think. French philosopher Rene Descartes (1596–1650 C.E.) compared the cry of an animal to the squeak of a clock spring, a mechanical reaction. Even in the modern era, animal behaviorists are reluctant to commit to the existence of complex emotions in animals for fear of being accused of anthropomorphism, ascribing human traits to nonhuman beings, and are belittled for being "unscientific" when they refer to an animal's inner life.

Which of the following quotes most logically supports the claim in the last sentence of the text?

(A) Scientist Philip Low says, "If you ask my colleagues whether animals have emotions and thoughts, many will drop their voices or change the subject."

(B) Scientist Philip Low says, "My cat meows plaintively every time I leave the house."

(C) Scientist Philip Low says, "Every day we learn more about animals' cognitive abilities, their emotional capacities, and their moral lives."

(D) Scientist Philip Low says, "Animal behavior can be easily explained in terms of the stimulus-response theory."

7. The following excerpt is from the 2022 Study Update from the Agricultural Health Study (AHS).

In some previous studies, agricultural work and occupational pesticide use have been associated with increased rates of renal cell carcinoma (RCC), the most common form of kidney cancer. However, few of those studies had investigated links to specific pesticides. Researchers evaluated associations with 38 pesticides, including one labeled 2,4,5-T, that were relatively commonly used at enrollment among pesticide applicators in the Agricultural Health Study, 308 individuals who developed RCC during follow-up until 2015. They hypothesized that certain pesticides, including and other agricultural exposure might influence the development of kidney disease and kidney cancer.

Which of the findings, if true, would directly support the researchers' hypothesis?

(A) Farmers and agricultural workers face health risks from work-related injuries at a rate of 18 deaths per 100,00 workers.

(B) Farmers and agricultural workers face stress from environmental factors, such as droughts, floods, wildfires, pests, and diseases affecting crops and livestock, as well as from working long hours, financial concerns, and feelings of isolation and frustration.

(C) Farmers and agricultural workers who use methods of organic food production (avoiding artificial fertilizers and pesticides and using crop rotation and other forms of husbandry to maintain soil fertility, control weeds and diseases) were less likely to report incidences of cancer.

(D) Farmers and agricultural workers who use the herbicide 2,4,5-T were three times more likely to develop RCC compared with those who never used this product.

8.

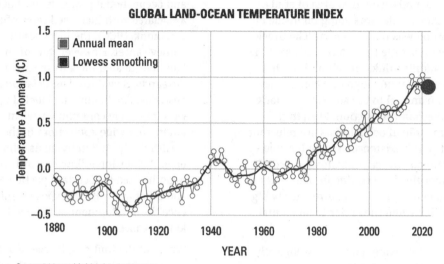

GLOBAL LAND-OCEAN TEMPERATURE INDEX

Source: https://climate.nasa.gov

Lowess smoothing (Locally Weighted Scatterplot Smoothing) is a tool used in data analysis that creates a smooth line through a time plot or scatter plot to help you to see a relationship between variables and predict trends.

Among environmental scientists, there is a strong consensus that global surface temperatures have increased in recent decades and that the trend is caused by human-induced emissions of greenhouse gases. The extra energy that results from human activities has warmed the atmosphere, ocean, and land, and widespread and rapid changes in the atmosphere, ocean, cryosphere, and biosphere have occurred. The actual warming of temperatures is something they say they can document. In fact, according to an intergovernmental panel on climate change, the scientific evidence that points to climate change is undeniable.

Which of the following findings, if true, would appear to weaken the conclusion of the intergovernmental panel?

(A) The global mean sea levels have doubled compared to the 20th-century trend of 1.6 mm per year, and this is accelerating slightly every year. The global sea levels rose about 8 inches in the last century.

(B) The increased heat in the atmosphere from greenhouse gas emissions has been absorbed by the oceans, with the top 700 meters (about 2,300 feet) of ocean showing warming of more than 0.4 degree Fahrenheit since 1969.

(C) Core measures of the Arctic ice show that it has increased in volume since 2012 — by 50 percent in 2012 alone.

(D) Tracking global atmospheric temperatures since the 1800s, scientists point to a steady rise with a stronger period in the 1970s, a lull in the 1990s, and a return to the rising pattern in the 2000s.

9. A tornado is a narrow, violently rotating column of air _____ from a thunderstorm to the ground. Because wind is invisible, it is hard to see a tornado unless it forms a condensation funnel made up of water droplets, dust, and debris. Tornadoes can be among the most violent phenomena of all atmospheric storms we experience.

Which of the following completes the text so that it conforms to the conventions of Standard English?

(A) that extend

(B) by which it extends

(C) that extends

(D) in which it extends

10. Some sugars used by manufacturers in foods and drinks that you buy may be different from what you traditionally think of as sugar, like sucrose or table sugar. These sugars meet the chemical definition of a _____ metabolized, or used by your body, differently than traditional sugars like sucrose.

Which of the following completes the text so that it conforms to the conventions of Standard English?

(A) sugar, which they are

(B) sugar, so it is

(C) sugar, and it is

(D) sugar, but they are

11. When I was growing up, my family always went to a lake in the Adirondack Mountains for a week of camping. My brothers and _____ would spend hours fishing, swimming, and searching for tadpoles in the lake.

Which of the following completes the text so that it conforms to the conventions of Standard English?

(A) we

(B) me

(C) I

(D) them

12. Our planet Earth is composed of several layers. Each layer has a unique density (density = mass/volume). Scientists believe that all planets formed on the basis of _____ the layering of Earth is a result of gravitational pull. The densest layer (inner core) is at the center and the least dense layer (crust) is the outermost layer. The atmosphere, composed of gases, can technically be considered a layer as well and is obviously lighter than the crust.

Which of the following completes the text with the most logical transition?

(A) gravity; therefore,

(B) gravity; however,

(C) gravity, but

(D) gravity; instead,

13. While researching a topic, a student has taken the following notes:

- The density of Jupiter is 1.326g/cm³.

- Jupiter is larger than any other planet in the solar system.

- The stripes and swirls on the surface of Jupiter are cold, windy clouds of ammonia and water.

- The density of Saturn is 0.687g/cm³.

- Saturn has the most complicated rings — primarily chunks of ice — of any planet.

- Saturn is a massive ball made mostly of hydrogen and helium.

The student wants to compare the size of the two planets. Which choice most effectively uses relevant information from the notes to accomplish this goal?

(A) Some of the planets in the solar system like Jupiter and Saturn are mostly composed of gases.

(B) Both Saturn and Jupiter have distinctive surface features which have been captured in images taken by NASA spacecraft.

(C) Although both Saturn and Jupiter are composed of similar gases, Jupiter is bigger and denser than Saturn.

(D) Saturn's rings are composed mostly of chunks of ice while Jupiter's distinctive stripes and swirls are clouds.

14. While researching a topic, a student has taken the following notes:

- Robert Frost wrote the poem, "Nothing Gold Can Stay" (1923), about how quickly things in nature fade.

- Frost often wrote about scenes from rural life in New England.

- The poem, "Nothing Gold Can Stay," was published in a collection called *New Hampshire* the same year (1923), which would later win the 1924 Pulitzer Prize.

- In "Nothing Gold Can Stay," Frost applies the images of nature to the larger themes such as the passage of time.

- Frost draws a parallel from nature to the short-lived quality of beauty, youth, and life in "Nothing Gold Can Stay."

The student wants to create a statement that will introduce the poet and his major themes to an audience unfamiliar with Robert Frost. Which choice most effectively uses information from the notes to accomplish this task?

(A) Pulitzer Prize–winning poet Robert Frost often uses nature images from rural New England to express themes about nature and human existence.

(B) Robert Frost wrote "Nothing Gold Can Stay" in 1923, and the collection of poems that it was published in won a Pulitzer Prize.

(C) "Nothing Gold Can Stay," written by Robert Frost in 1923, is about the fleeting quality of nature, youth, and time.

(D) Robert Frost, who wrote many poems, is famous for his poems about life and nature.

Check your work.

Continue to the next module when you're ready to move on.

Section 2: Math

Module 1

TIME: 18 minutes for 11 questions.

DIRECTIONS: For multiple-choice questions, choose only one answer for each question. For fill-in questions, write only one answer, even if you find more than one correct answer. Don't include symbols such as a percent sign, comma, or dollar sign.

NOTES:

- All numbers used in this exam are real numbers.

- All figures lie in a plane.

- All figures may be assumed to be to scale unless the problem specifically indicates otherwise.

- The domain of a given function f is the set of all real numbers x for which $f(x)$ is a real number, unless the problem specifically indicates otherwise.

- You may use a calculator.

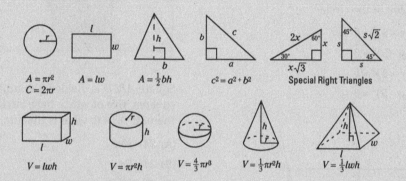

$A = \pi r^2$
$C = 2\pi r$
$A = lw$
$A = \frac{1}{2}bh$
$c^2 = a^2 + b^2$
Special Right Triangles

$V = lwh$
$V = \pi r^2 h$
$V = \frac{4}{3}\pi r^3$
$V = \frac{1}{3}\pi r^2 h$
$V = \frac{1}{3}lwh$

- The number of degrees in a circle is 360.

- The number of radians in a circle is 2π.

- The sum of the measures of the angles of a triangle is 180.

1. In the xy-coordinate plane, what is the area of the rectangle with opposite vertices at $(-3,-1)$ and $(3,1)$?

   (A) 3
   (B) 6
   (C) 9
   (D) 12

2. If $\frac{4}{5}$ of a number is 24, what is $\frac{1}{5}$ of the number?

   (A) 5
   (B) 6
   (C) 8
   (D) 18

3. A circle in the xy-coordinate plane has a center of $(2, 5)$ and a radius of 3. Which of the following is an equation of the circle?

   (A) $(x-2)^2 +(y-5)^2 = 9$
   (B) $(x-2)^2 +(y-5)^2 = 3$
   (C) $(x+2)^2 -(y+5)^2 = 9$
   (D) $(x+2)^2 -(y+5)^2 = 3$

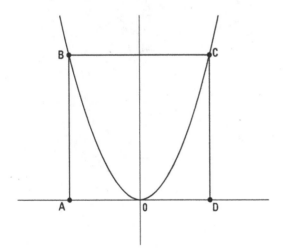

4. How much greater than $t-5$ is $t+2$?

   (A) 2
   (B) 4
   (C) 5
   (D) 7

5. The price of a television was first decreased by 10 percent and then increased by 20 percent. The final price was what percent of the initial price?

   (A) 88%
   (B) 90%
   (C) 98%
   (D) 108%

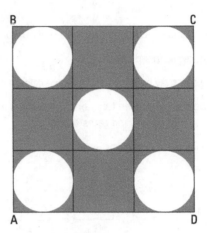

6. Square ABCD is divided into nine equal squares, five of which have circles inscribed in them. If $AB = 6$, what is the total shaded area?

   (A) $24-10\pi$
   (B) $24-5\pi$
   (C) $36-10\pi$
   (D) $36-5\pi$

7. In the xy-plane, line l passes through $(-1,3)$ and is parallel to the line $4x+2y = k$. If line l passes through the point $(p,-p)$, what is the value of p?

   (A) −2
   (B) −1
   (C) 1
   (D) 2

8. $y = x^2 - 2x + 3$
   $y = -3x + 5$

   How many solutions are there to the system of equations above?

   (A) The answer cannot be determined with the information given.
   (B) There are no solutions.
   (C) There is exactly one solution.
   (D) There are exactly two solutions.

9. A certain fraction is equivalent to $\frac{2}{3}$. If the fraction's denominator is 12 less than twice its numerator, find the denominator of the fraction.

10. If $x^2 - 3x = 50$ and $x^2 + 5x = 12$, what is the value of $x^2 + x$?

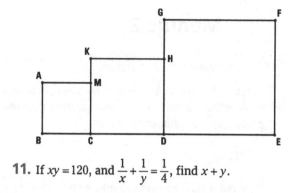

11. If $xy = 120$, and $\frac{1}{x} + \frac{1}{y} = \frac{1}{4}$, find $x + y$.

Check your work.

Continue to the next module when you're ready to move on.

Module 2

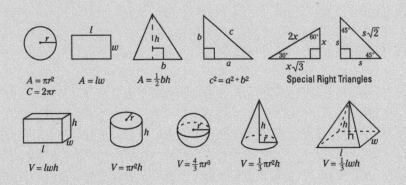

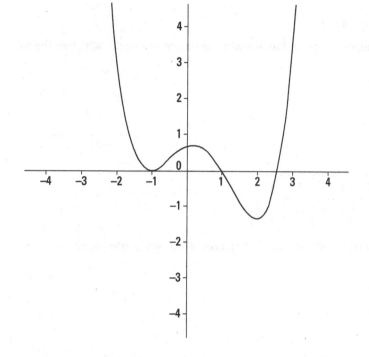

1. The preceding figure shows the graph of
   $y = f(x)$ from $x = -3$ to $x = 4$. For what value of
   x in this interval does the function f attain its
   minimum value?

   (A) 2

   (B) 1

   (C) 0

   (D) −2

2. If $-1 < x < 0$, which of the following statements
   must be true?

   I. $x > \dfrac{x}{2}$

   II. $x^2 > x$

   III. $x^3 > x^2$

   (A) I only

   (B) II only

   (C) I and II only

   (D) II and III only

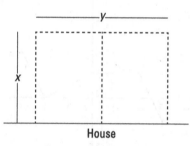

House

3. A gardener is building a fence to enclose their
   garden and divide it in half, as shown in the
   preceding figure. The fourth side of the garden is adjacent to their house, so it does not
   require fencing. The total area of the garden
   is 2,400 square feet. In terms of x, how many
   feet of fencing does the gardener require?

   (A) $2,400 - 3x$

   (B) $x + \dfrac{2,400}{x}$

   (C) $3x + \dfrac{2,400}{x}$

   (D) $3x + \dfrac{1,200}{x}$

GO ON TO NEXT PAGE

4. $x^2 + y^2 - 4x - 6y + 12 = 0$

In the xy-plane, the graph of the preceding equation is a circle. Which of the following is the radius of the circle?

(A) 4

(B) 3

(C) 2

(D) 1

k	1	2	3	4	5	6
$f(k)$	15	11	7	n	−1	−5

5. The preceding table defines a linear function. What is the value of n?

(A) 1

(B) 2

(C) 3

(D) 4

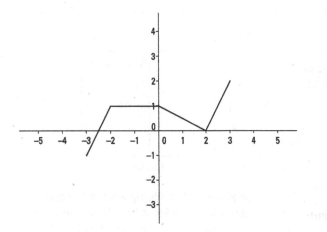

6. The graph of $y = g(x)$ is shown above. Which of the following could be the graph of $y = g(x-1)$?

(A)

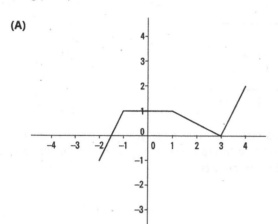

(B)

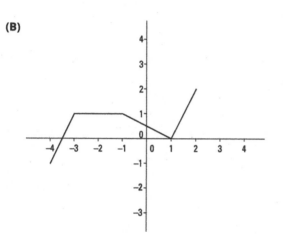

(C)

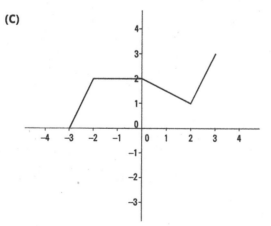

(D)

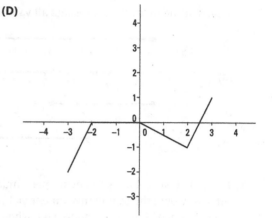

7. In the xy-plane, lines p and q are perpendicular. If line p contains the points $(-2, 2)$ and $(2, 1)$, and line q contains the points $(-2, 4)$ and $(k, 0)$, what is the value of k?

(A) -3

(B) -2

(C) -1

(D) 0

8. If $a = \dfrac{1}{2}$ in the preceding equation, what is the value of b?

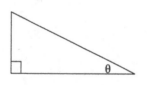

9. In the right triangle shown above, if angle $\theta = 30°$, what is $\sin\theta$?

10. Which of the following represents all values of x that satisfy this inequality: $7 \geq -2x + 3$?

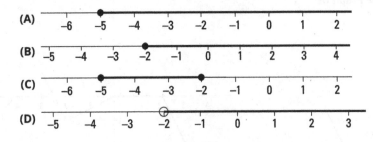

11. If $1,000 invested at i percent simple annual interest yields $200 over a 2-year period, how much interest would the $1,000 investment yield if the i percent interest were compounded annually over the 2-year period? Ignore the dollar sign when filling in your answer.

Check your work.

Answers and Explanations

After you finish the practice test sections, take some time to go through the answers and explanations in this section to find out which questions you missed and why. Even if you answered the question correctly, the explanation may offer a useful strategy that speeds up your performance on the next round. The explanations include additional information that'll be useful on the real SAT. If you're short on time, turn to the end of this section to find an abbreviated answer key.

Section 1: Reading and Writing

Module 1

1. **C.** A mailman delivering your mail in a horse-drawn cart would be out of date, no longer in use, or **obsolete**. Choice C is the best answer.

2. **D.** The text suggests that to counter the threat to natural resources, incentives will **encourage** landowners to use sustainable management. While Choice C is tempting because it is a positive word, you should take the time to put the words into the sentence and reread it to find the **best** choice. The context clue *incentive* should lead you to choose **encourage**. Choice D is the best answer for the context.

3. **A.** The text states that "bison were nearly driven to extinction through uncontrolled hunting and a U.S. policy of eradication." This context clue should lead you to Choice A, **persecution** (hostility and ill treatment).

4. **C.** The passage states that Amelia Earhart "maintained an attitude of impenetrable mediocrity," and that's what got her the job. That phrase should lead you to select Choice C, opaque (impenetrable) and ordinariness (averageness or mediocrity). Don't allow words in the text like "curious," "demure," and "respectful" to tempt you to choose the incorrect answer Choices B or D. While those choices are used in the text to describe Earhart, they are not the qualities that got her the job.

5. **A.** In these lines, the speaker in the poem claims that "you" (the person being addressed) see in "me" (the speaker) someone nearing the end of his life ("on the ashes of his youth doth lie"). You see this ("This thou perceivest") and that makes you love me more ("makes thy love more strong"). Thus, the knowledge that the speaker will soon die drives the partner to love him even more. No evidence in the poem supports the other choices. Choice A is the best answer.

6. **D.** The sentence that best concludes the text is one that sums up the brief biography of Deb Haaland. Choices A, B, and C offer more details about Secretary Haaland's life. Only Choice D offers a summary of Secretary Haaland's life and her accomplishments thus far.

7. **D.** The "insignificant" marks left by the plow indicate that it is a primitive implement that leaves a trail similar to the "feeble" marks left by prehistoric people. This comparison with prehistoric people creates a picture of a very early and somewhat ineffectual form of farming. Choice D is the best statement of the purpose of this line in the text.

8. **D.** The past perfect form of the verb is needed to show action that occurred in the past over a period of time. Choice A is incorrect because *begun* can only be used as a verb in conjunction with a form of the verb *to have*. Choice B is incorrect because the correct form of the verb to use with *had* is the past participle *begun*. Choice C is incorrect because *has begun* is the present perfect tense, and the war took place in the past.

9. **A.** Choice A uses the correctly spelled *there* and the correct plural form of the verb *were* to agree with the plural noun *rabbits.* Choice B incorrectly uses the singular form of the verb *was.* Choice C uses the incorrect word *their.* Choice D incorrectly uses *they're*, the contraction of *they are.*

10. **A.** Choice A uses the correct correlative conjunction *or* (remember the pairs: *either–or, neither–nor*) and the correct mark of punctuation, the semicolon, to join two independent clauses. Choice B has the dreaded comma splice error! Never use a comma to connect two independent clauses! Choice C and D incorrectly use *nor* rather than *or.*

11. **A.** Choice A correctly uses the colon after a main clause before information that clarifies the main clause. The other choices are incorrectly punctuated.

12. **D.** Choice D correctly uses the singular possessive pronoun *its* to refer to his design for the entrance to the Louvre. Choice A incorrectly uses the plural pronoun *their.* Choice B incorrectly uses *it's*, the contraction of *it is.* Choice C incorrectly adds an apostrophe to the possessive pronoun *its.* (A possessive pronoun never has an apostrophe because it is already possessive!)

13. **B.** Choice B correctly uses the transitional word *Indeed* to add emphasis to the point of the second sentence, which agrees with and extends the idea of the lack of knowledge of the Greeks. Choices A, C, and D incorrectly use contrast words.

14. **C.** Choice C is the best answer because it highlights the distinguishing character qualities of Elizabeth Blackwell, which is what the prompt asks you to consider when selecting a choice. While Choices A, B, and D are true, they do not emphasize Blackwell's distinguishing qualities.

Module 2

1. **C.** Choice C, **contrived to**, is the best choice to fit into the context of the sentence. The Egyptians **contrived** (created or managed to do something) a method of tempering iron ore so that they could shape it into tools and weapons. Choices A and B suggest the Egyptians didn't want to make tools and weapons, which is illogical based on the text. Choice D doesn't make logical sense.

2. **A.** The logic of the context suggests that the new, lower-cost method is preferable to the current method, which is costly and **requires** the help of experts (which would add to the cost and make it less user-friendly). None of the other choices are logical in the context of the sentences.

3. **D.** Choice D is the best choice because, beginning with the word *Hence* (which means *for this reason*), it presents a statement of what will happen as a result of the previously described situation. The underlined text draws a logical conclusion from the information in the previous sentences. It isn't a specific example (Choice A) or a new idea (Choice B) that counters a previously accepted conclusion. It doesn't provide further detail about any particular species (Choice C).

4. **A.** Choice A is the best choice because the underlined sentence clarifies the meaning of *non-native.* It doesn't offer a specific example, so Choice B is incorrect. Choice C is incorrect because it doesn't offer an exception. Choice D is incorrect because there is no counterclaim.

5. **B.** The City School Superintendent concluded that most schools in the district were consistently providing a health education course in all grades of secondary school. However, according to the data, less than 25 percent of the schools offered students in grades 10 through 12 a health education course as compared to close to 75 percent of the schools in grades 6 through 9. This data clearly weakens the Superintendent's conclusion. Nothing in the data supports the other choices.

6. **A.** According to the text, most animal behaviorists are unwilling to admit that animals have thoughts and feelings. (Dog and cat lovers among us know differently!) Choice A most accurately reflects the current thinking about attributing emotions and thoughts to animals. Choice B is off topic. Choice C, while it may be true, isn't supported by the text. Choice D is also somewhat off topic.

7. **D.** The evidence that farmers who use a herbicide are three times more likely to develop renal cell carcinoma supports the conclusion that certain pesticides (including the herbicide 2.4.5-T) lead to the development of kidney disease and kidney cancer. Choice A is too general to support the claim. Choice B is off topic. Choice C is also off topic.

8. **C.** If it is true that Arctic ice increased in volume by 50 percent in 2012 alone, this statistic would appear to weaken the conclusion that the evidence pointing to climate change is undeniable. A decrease in the Artic ice core is often used as a measurement of global warming. Choices A, B, and D all support, not weaken the conclusion of the panel.

9. **C.** Choice C completes the text with the most concise and grammatically correct phrase *that extends.* The subject of the verb *extends* is a singular noun, *tornado,* which agrees with the singular form of the verb *extends.* Choice A is incorrect because it uses the plural form of the verb *extend,* which doesn't agree with the singular subject *tornado.* Choice B is both wordy and inaccurate; the air is not the method *by which* the tornado extends. The tornado is the air. Choice D is also wordy and inaccurate: The tornado doesn't extend *in* the air; it *is* the air.

10. **D.** Choice D is the most logical and grammatically correct choice to complete the sentence. First, Choice D uses the correct plural pronoun *they* to refer to the plural subject *sugars.* Choices B and C incorrectly use the singular pronoun *it* to refer to the plural subject *sugars.* Choice A uses the correct pronoun *they,* but it uses the ungrammatical and illogical wording *which they are metabolized* instead of the conjunction *but + they are* to show the contrast between the ways these sugars are metabolized.

11. **C.** This is a tricky case of pronoun case! *I* is a subject pronoun (nominative case) and *me* is an object pronoun (objective case); they are never interchangeable! If the pronoun is a doer (as in *I* would spend hours fishing . . .), then you always use the subject pronoun. If the pronoun receives the action (my brother handed *me* the rod), then you always use the object pronoun . . . not so tricky now, right? The only correct pronoun in the choices is Choice C.

12. **A.** The logical relationship between the first half of the sentence and the second half is cause and effect. The best word to indicate that the layering is a result of gravity is *therefore.* Gravity (the cause) creates layering (the result). Choices B, C, and D, *however, but,* and *instead,* all indicate a contrast, which does not conform to the logic of the sentence.

13. **C.** In this question, your careful reading of the prompt is very important. (Actually, it always is!) Your task is to choose relevant information from the notes to compare the sizes of the planets, so all the other information in the notes is not relevant to your choice. Choice C is the best choice because it uses relevant information (not all the information) to make a comparison between the sizes of Saturn and Jupiter. All the other choices contain true — but irrelevant — information.

14. **A.** Choice A most effectively introduces the poet and his major themes to an audience unfamiliar with Robert Frost. (Hard to imagine!) None of the other choices include all the important information, and none are written as effectively as Choice A.

Section 2: Math

Module 1

1. **D.** Sketch out this problem to help you solve it:

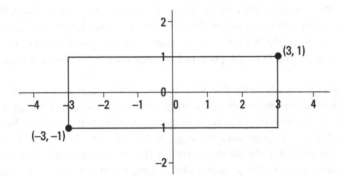

The length of the rectangle is 6, and the height is 2. The area of a rectangle is *length* times *width*, so the area of this rectangle is $(6)(2) = 12$.

2. **B.** Set up the equation with x as the number and solve for x.

$$\frac{4}{5}x = 24$$
$$4x = 120$$
$$x = 30$$

Now find $\frac{1}{5}$ of 30, which is 6.

3. **A.** The equation for a circle is $(x - h)^2 + (y - k)^2 = r^2$, where h, k, and r are the x- and y-coordinates of the center and r is the radius. Place these coordinates and radius 2, 5, and 3 for h, k, and r, respectively, in the equation for $(x - 2)^2 + (y - 5)^2 = 3^2$ and square the 3 on the end. Choice (A) matches this answer.

4. **D.** Get rid of the t, and the question becomes, "How much greater than -5 is 2?" Well, that would be 7, so Choice (D) is the right answer.

5. **D.** Whenever you're working on percentage problems, it's a great idea to start with $100. So if the TV cost $100, and then the price was decreased by 10 percent ($10), the reduced price is $90. You add 20 percent on to 90 by finding 20 percent of 90 and adding it to $90: $0.20(90) = 18$; $90 + $18 = 108. It's easy to see that $108 is 108 percent of $100: $\frac{\$108}{\$100} = 1.08 = 108\%$.

6. **D.** The first step is to find the area of square $ABCD$. You know the length of one of the sides, so you know that the area is that length squared: $6^2 = 36$. Now you just need to subtract off the area of the five circles. You can see that each of the nine smaller squares has a side length equal to one-third of the length of the big square: $\frac{1}{3}(6) = 2$. This means that each circle has a diameter of 2 and a radius of 1. The area of a circle is $A = \pi r^2$, so the area of each circle is $A = \pi(1)^2 = \pi$. Now you can find the area of the shaded part of the diagram. The area will be the total square area minus the area of five circles: $36 - 5\pi$, or Choice (D).

7. **C.** The first step is to find the slope of the given line by solving for y:

$$2y = -4x + k$$
$$y = -2x + \frac{k}{2}$$

The slope of this line is -2. Because you know that line l is parallel to this line, you now know that line l has a slope of -2. Now you can use the point $(-1, 3)$ and $y = mx + b$ to determine the equation of l. Substitute -2 for m, -1 for x, and 3 for y, and then solve for b: $3 = -2(-1) + b$, so $b = 1$. Now you know the equation for l is $y = -2x + 1$. You can substitute p and $-p$ in for x and y, respectively, to solve the problem: $-p = -2(p) + 1$. Simplifying, $-p = -2p + 1$, or $p = 1$.

8. **D.** The number of solutions as graphed means how many times do the two functions cross, but in algebra it refers to the number of possible values of x. Since each expression is equal to y, set the expressions equal to each other:

$$x^2 - 2x + 3 = -3x + 5$$
$$x^2 + x - 2 = 0$$
$$(x + 2)(x - 1) = 0$$

Looks like x has two solutions.

9. **36.** If the numerator is n, the denominator is $2n - 12$. Start by finding the numerator:

$$\frac{2}{3} = \frac{n}{2n - 12}$$
$$2(2n - 12) = 3n$$
$$4n - 24 = 3n$$
$$n = 24$$

Hold on, though — n is the *numerator*, but you need the *denominator*. You know that the fraction is equivalent to $\frac{2}{3}$, so set up the equation with d as the denominator:

$$\frac{2}{3} = \frac{24}{d}$$
$$2d = 72$$
$$d = 36$$

10. **31.** Don't math it out. You *could* solve for x and place the value into $x^2 + x$, but because this is the SAT, you know there's an easier way. First add the two equations:

$$x^2 - 3x = 50$$
$$+(x^2 + 5x = 12)$$
$$\overline{2x^2 + 2x = 62}$$

Divide both sides by 2, and $x^2 + x = 31$.

11. 30. This question is all about working with fractions. Consider the following:

$$\frac{1}{x} + \frac{1}{y} = \frac{1}{4}$$

When you're working with fractions, getting a common denominator on each side is a good idea. Here's how it works out:

$$\left(\frac{y}{y}\right)\frac{1}{x} + \left(\frac{x}{x}\right)\frac{1}{y} = \frac{1}{4}$$

$$\frac{y}{xy} + \frac{x}{xy} = \frac{1}{4}$$

$$\frac{x+y}{xy} = \frac{1}{4}$$

You know that $xy = 120$, so plug that in and solve for $x + y$ as a single unit (in other words, not x and y separately).

$$\frac{x+y}{xy} = \frac{1}{4}$$

$$\frac{x+y}{(120)} = \frac{1}{4}$$

$$4(x+y) = 120$$

$$x+y = 30$$

Module 2

1. A. The minimum value of a function is where the y-value is the lowest. Find the lowest point of the curve, and check the x-value: The y-value is lowest where x is 2.

2. B. This problem is easier if you pick a number for x, such as -0.5 or $-\frac{1}{2}$, and try out each statement. Try the first statement:

$$-0.5 > \frac{-0.5}{2}$$
$$-0.5 > -0.25$$

This is false, so eliminate Choices (A) and (C). Choices (B) and (D) both claim that Statement II is true, but try it just to be sure:

$$(-0.5)^2 > -0.5$$
$$0.25 > -0.5$$

This is true, so now check Statement III for the tiebreaker:

$$(-0.5)^3 > (-0.5)^2$$
$$-0.125 > 0.25$$

And it's not true. Choice (B) is the answer.

3. C. The fence that the gardener needs is equal to $3x + y$, so what you really need to do is figure out a way to represent y in terms of x. Because the area of the garden is 2,400 square feet, you can use your knowledge of the area of a rectangle to see that $2,400 = xy$. Divide both sides by x to solve for y for $y = \frac{2,400}{x}$, and then place that back in to the original expression for the total fencing needed: $3x + y = 3x + \frac{2,400}{x}$, Choice (C).

4. **D.** Convert the equation of the circle to the center-radius form, where the center is (h, k) and the radius is r: $(x-h)^2 + (y-k)^2 = r^2$.

$$x^2 + y^2 - 4x - 6y + 12 = 0$$
$$x^2 + y^2 - 4x - 6y = -12$$
$$\left[x^2 - 4x\right] + \left[y^2 - 6y\right] = -12$$
$$\left[(x-2)^2 - 4\right] + \left[(y-3)^2 - 9\right] = -12$$
$$(x-2)^2 + (y-3)^2 = 1$$

Because $r^2 = 1$, $r = 1$ and the answer is Choice (D).

5. **C.** Looking at the chart, you can see that the top row increases by one in each box. In the bottom row, each box is four fewer than the previous one. That means that n will be four fewer than 7, or n is $7 - 4 = 3$.

6. **A.** When you change the x-value in a function, the graph changes horizontally. In this case, you're subtracting 1 from x before plugging it into the function g, so the graph shifts either left or right. Knowing this narrows your choices down to Choices (A) and (B). You can look at the original graph and see that $g(2) = 0$. To get $y = g(x - 1)$ to equal 0, you need $x - 1$ to equal 2: $x - 1 = 2$, $x = 3$. That means that $(3, 0)$ will be a point on the transformed graph. Choice (A) is the only graph with that point on it.

7. **A.** Your first step is to find the slope of line p.

$$m = \frac{2-1}{-2-2} = \frac{1}{-4} = -\frac{1}{4}$$

Because perpendicular lines have opposite (negative) reciprocal slopes, the slope of line q must be 4. So far, you know that line q has a slope of 4 and passes through the point $(-2, 4)$. You can use the equation $y = 4x + b$ and substitute in the point to figure out what b is: $4 = 4(-2) + b$ becomes $b = 12$ when you solve it. Now you have the equation of line q: $y = 4x + 12$. Substitute in the point $(k, 0)$ and solve for k: $0 = 4k + 12$, $-12 = 4k$, and $k = -3$.

8. **17.** Place $\frac{1}{2}$ for a and solve for b:

$$a - \frac{1}{2}b = -8$$
$$\left(\frac{1}{2}\right) - \frac{1}{2}b = -8$$
$$-\frac{1}{2}b = -8\frac{1}{2}$$
$$b = 17$$

9. $\frac{1}{2}$ **or 0.5.** If one angle is 90° and angle $\theta = 30°$, then the third angle is 60°, making this a 30-60-90 triangle with a side ratio of $1 : \sqrt{3} : 2$. The sine of an angle is the angle's opposite side, which in this case is the triangle's smallest side, over the triangle's hypotenuse. From the ratio, you know that the smallest side is half the length of the hypotenuse, for an answer of $\frac{1}{2}$ or 0.5. When you grid in your answer, either $\frac{1}{2}$ or 0.5 is considered correct.

10. B. Simplify the expression. Just remember that when you divide both sides by a negative (in this case, –2), you switch the inequality sign. Then you swap the x and the value, meaning you switch the inequality sign again:

$$7 \geq -2x + 3$$
$$4 \geq -2x$$
$$-2 \leq x$$
$$x \geq -2$$

Both Choices (B) and (D) include numbers greater than –2, but Choice (B) has the circle at –2 filled in, meaning that –2 is included in the solution set, which is exactly what you want because you're looking for all numbers greater than or *equal to* –2.

11. 210. If $1,000 invested at i percent simple annual interest yields $200 over a two-year period, you can deduce that it earns $100 over one year. To find i, the interest rate, yielding $100 simple annual interest on $1,000, divide the amount of interest by the amount of the investment:

$$\frac{100}{1,000} = 0.1 = 10\%$$

Now you know that $i = 10$, for an interest rate of 10 percent.

To calculate compound interest, you can use the compound interest formula. However, for only two cycles, you can find the answer without the formula. Simply calculate the simple interest twice: once for the first year, and once for the second year. Start with the original $1,000 investment, and increase it 10 percent:

$$\$1,000 + (10\% \times \$1,000) = \$1,000 + \$100 = \$1,100$$

The investment is worth $1,100 at the end of the first year. To find its value at the end of the second year, increase $1,100 by 10 percent:

$$\$1,100 + (10\% \times \$1,100) = \$1,100 + \$110 = \$1,210$$

The question asks for the amount of interest yielded, not the final value. To find the amount of interest, subtract the original value from the final value:

$$\$1,210 - \$1,000 = \$210$$

Answer Key

Section 1: Reading and Writing, Module 1

1.	C	5.	A	9.	A	13.	B
2.	D	6.	D	10.	A	14.	C
3.	A	7.	D	11.	A		
4.	C	8.	D	12.	D		

Section 2: Reading and Writing, Module 2

1.	C	5.	B	9.	C	13.	C
2.	A	6.	A	10.	D	14.	A
3.	D	7.	D	11.	C		
4.	A	8.	C	12.	A		

Section 3: Math, Module 1

1.	D	4.	D	7.	C	10.	31
2.	B	5.	D	8.	D	11.	30
3.	A	6.	D	9.	36		

Section 4: Math, Module 2

1.	A	4.	D	7.	A	10.	B
2.	B	5.	C	8.	17	11.	210
3.	C	6.	A	9.	.5 or $\frac{1}{2}$		

Block 5

Ten Tips for the Night Before the SAT

Your SAT is tomorrow. Scared? That's normal. When you walk into that testing room, *everyone* is scared — except you're more prepared than they are. The fear is normal, so don't deny it. Just accept that tomorrow is a big day and do what you can to control it, starting with the night before test day.

REMEMBER

The key to success in any performance is to be well prepared and to go into the performance relaxed and confident. You already put in all the hard work to prepare yourself — you studied the topics in high school, reviewed the material, worked through this test-prep guide (and maybe others), answered sample questions, checked your work, and reviewed some more. That's all behind you. Doing any more brain-intensive work the night before is likely to be counterproductive. Now's the time to focus on being relaxed and confident. In this block, you find out how to do just that!

Give Your Brain a Break

Most important: *Don't study anything.* When's the last time somebody advised you *not* to study before a test? Don't get me wrong; studying to prepare for a test is important. Just don't do it the *night before* the test. At this stage in the game, your brain should be packed with all the knowledge and understanding necessary for you to perform well. Now you need to relax and be confident, so you can think clearly on test day.

Get your rest. You've prepared for months (or weeks), and you've built your skills and addressed your gaps. Right now, you need to build your strength and clear your mind, so *get some rest.* Now is the time to shift focus from studying to conserving energy and optimizing your mental clarity.

Stay Home and Healthy

Keeping your mind off the SAT the night before is always a good idea, but that doesn't mean it's party time. Plan a low-key evening, eat healthy, and avoid consuming anything that could disrupt your sleep or give you a bad case of brain fog in the morning. Here are a few specific suggestions:

>> Stay home or take a walk outside. Don't do anything very social.

>> Watch a comedy or do some light reading.

>> Eat a wholesome meal — whole foods, a little fat, a little protein, and mostly vegetables, with little to no heavy carbs like breads or pasta.

>> Avoid eating anything super-spicy or high in sugar. Spicy foods can give you indigestion in the morning, and carbs or sugar can make your brain surge and crash the next day.

>> Take your prescription medications, but don't consume anything that's going to impair your thinking or judgment or keep you from getting a good night's sleep.

REMEMBER

At this stage in your life, you know what you need to do the night before to wake up the next morning feeling rested and fresh, so do whatever that is.

Maintain a Positive Mindset

Most important, resist the urge to contact friends who are also taking the test. If they're nervous, their anxiety is going to feed your anxiety. Instead, *mitigate* (reduce the effect of) your anxiety by taking control of the situation and your thoughts. Here are a couple suggestions:

>> Get all your stuff together, as detailed in the following sections, and place it all in one spot, so it's ready to go and you're not worried about forgetting something.

WARNING

You're not allowed to bring a laptop or tablet. Nor can you bring scrap paper, books, or other school supplies (including rulers, compasses, and highlighters). Leave them behind. Also, no portable music devices. If your watch is a smartwatch, leave it at home. Bring your phone, but be sure it's turned completely off and put away during the exam.

>> Engage in meditation, mindfulness, or relaxation techniques to clear your mind and focus it totally on the present. Focus on your sensations, your breathing, your heartbeat . . . anything except the past or future.

Find Your Admission Ticket

Don't leave home without your admission ticket! Take a picture, print it, and email it to yourself so you have backup if you can't find one form of the ticket. Before leaving home, make sure you have your admission ticket with you and know where it is. Without your ticket, you can't get in, and you'll have to do this whole routine over again.

Check for Your Photo ID

The SAT accepts your driver's license, school ID, passport, or almost any other official document that includes your picture. The SAT doesn't accept your Social Security card, credit card, or anything without your picture. If you're not sure what to bring, ask your school counselor or check the College Board website at www.collegeboard.org.

Gather Your Water Bottle and Snacks

Bring a couple of chilled water bottles to drink during your breaks. Don't bring anything sugary like soda or juice, because you'll crash and get even more thirsty. If you want electrolytes, such as a smart water, make sure it's a drink that you've tried before. If it gives you a headache, you don't want to discover that on the day of the test.

Bring healthy snacks in your backpack, so you don't have to wait in the vending machine line for a lousy selection. You can eat during your break, and your water bottles can keep them cold.

After you arrive at the test center, take out what you need and stow the rest of the stuff in a backpack under your seat.

Practice Your Stress-Management Strategies

You'll probably feel nervous when you arrive at the test center. This is normal, and it's okay. If you're prepared, then after you start the exam, you'll realize that it's all the stuff that you practiced, and you should feel better. Try a couple of stretches and head shakes to chase away tension. During the exam, wriggle your feet and move your shoulders up and down whenever you feel yourself tightening up. If you roll your neck, be sure to close your eyes and not to face the other students so you don't risk a charge of cheating. And take a few deep breaths to calm yourself.

Plan to Dress in Layers

You can't predict what the temperature in a test center is going to be, so dress in layers. Schools tend to freeze the heck out of the testing rooms, so wear enough clothing to stay within your comfort zone. On the other hand, on any given day, a testing room can feel like a sauna. Be prepared for any contingency by dressing in layers. Wear a light, short-sleeved shirt with a heavier shirt over it and a sweater or sweatshirt on top. If you're too warm, you can always strip down.

REMEMBER

You may not be allowed to wear a jacket or a cap, but a sweater or sweatshirt is okay.

Set Your Alarm and Have a Backup

You're old enough to know the importance of setting an alarm and getting up and out of bed as soon as it goes off in the morning, but I'm going to remind you to set your alarm anyway. I'm also going to advise you to arrange for a backup — ask your parents or guardians or another reliable someone to be sure you're up in time. If you don't have someone you can rely on, set another alarm.

Review Your Travel Plans to the Test Center

Make sure you have everything in place to ensure that you'll reach the test center with plenty of time to check in. By everything, I mean the following:

>> **A reliable means of transportation:** How are you planning to get to the test center — driving yourself, getting a ride, or using public transportation or a ride-sharing service? If you're driving your own car, make sure it starts and has plenty of gas. If someone's driving you, confirm your arrangements the night before.

>> **A clear route to the test center:** Check the route the night before and when you wake up in the morning to avoid getting thrown off schedule by traffic delays (accidents or construction).

>> **Estimated times of departure and arrival that leave plenty of room for the unexpected.** Plan to arrive at the test center 30 minutes early, so you have time to check in and get situated. You don't want to be stressed out just before the test begins.

Index

About the Authors

Ron Woldoff completed his dual master's degrees at Arizona State University and San Diego State University, where he studied the culmination of business and technology. After several years as a corporate consultant, Ron opened his own company, National Test Prep, where he has helped students reach their goals on the GMAT, GRE, SAT, ACT, and PSAT. He created the programs and curricula for these tests from scratch, using his own observations of the tests and feedback from students. Ron has also taught his own GMAT and GRE programs as an adjunct instructor at both Northern Arizona University and the internationally acclaimed Thunderbird School of Global Management, as well as SAT and ACT at various high schools. Ron lives in Phoenix, Arizona, with his lovely wife, Leisah, and their three amazing boys, Zachary, Jadon, and Adam. You can find Ron on the web at http://testprepaz.com.

Jane R. Burstein has decades of experience as an English teacher, adjunct professor, Advanced Placement (AP) reader, and tutor for the SAT, ACT, GRE, and GMAT exams. She is the author and coauthor of numerous English and test-prep books.

Publisher's Acknowledgments

Executive Editor: Lindsay Lefevere

Compiling Editor: Joe Kraynak

Editor: Elizabeth Kuball

Production Editor: Tamilmani Varadharaj

Cover Design: Wiley

Cover Image: © bortonia/Getty Images